CASS R. SUNSTEIN **/ Infotopia**

/ How Many Minds Produce Knowledge /

OXFORD
UNIVERSITY PRESS

2006

OXFORD
UNIVERSITY PRESS

Oxford University Press, Inc., publishes works that further
Oxford University's objective of excellence
in research, scholarship, and education.

Oxford   New York
Auckland   Cape Town   Dar es Salaam   Hong Kong   Karachi
Kuala Lumpur   Madrid   Melbourne   Mexico City   Nairobi
New Delhi   Shanghai   Taipei   Toronto

With offices in
Argentina   Austria   Brazil   Chile   Czech Republic   France   Greece
Guatemala   Hungary   Italy   Japan   Poland   Portugal   Singapore
South Korea   Switzerland   Thailand   Turkey   Ukraine   Vietnam

Published by Oxford University Press, Inc.
198 Madison Avenue, New York, New York 10016

www.oup.com

Library of Congress Cataloging-in-Publication Data
Sunstein, Cass R.
Infotopia : how many minds produce knowledge / Cass R. Sunstein.
p.   cm.
ISBN 978-0-19-518928-5
1. Personal information management.   2. Knowledge management.
3. Internet.   I. Title.
HD30.2.S85 2006
303.48'33—dc22   2005036052

9 8 7 6 5 4

Printed in the United States of America
on acid-free paper

For Leon Wieseltier

Preface and Acknowledgments /

Every day of every year, each of us relies on information that is provided by others. Even the most informed people have direct knowledge of only a tiny fraction of the "facts" on which their lives depend. When we choose what to eat and where to go, what to trust and what to fear, we make use of information that is conveyed to us by other human beings. It is hard to overstate the importance of this fact, which is responsible for many of humanity's greatest errors and largest successes. A major question is this: Is there a way for all of us to know what each of us knows? And is it possible to find such a way without eliminating the incentive to learn more?

Much of my focus in this book is on deliberation, an ancient form of interaction that will undoubtedly continue as long as the human race. I emphasize that if we all want to learn what each of us knows, deliberation is full of pitfalls. Deliberating groups can blunder badly; sometimes they act like mobs. One of my primary goals is to outline the dangers and to show why they are likely to cause serious trouble if we are not alert to them.

I also explore the nature and implications of new and, in some ways, revolutionary methods for aggregating the information held by many minds. These methods are facilitated, or even made possible, by the Internet: prediction markets, wikis, open source software, and blogs. Prediction markets can be substitutes for deliberation, or at least valuable complements. Wikis and open source software may or may not involve deliberation; in any case, they have exceptionable promise. The world of blogs is full of deliberation, and the blogosphere benefits from the views and thoughts of countless minds. But it runs into the usual pitfalls that undermine deliberation, sometimes in heightened forms.

At their best, the new methods have two remarkable virtues. First, they show us fresh ways to obtain access to the information held by many minds. Second, they show us how we might dramatically improve the old method of deliberation by increasing the likelihood that groups can learn what their members know. Access to many minds contains risks, because many people can and do blunder. But for society's most important institutions, dispersed information, if elicited, is far more likely to lead to better understanding— and ultimately to more sensible decisions in both markets and politics.

This short book has been long in coming. Its development has been an effort to vindicate the claim that products are likely to be a lot better if information is properly aggregated from numerous and diverse minds. Versions of this book were presented as the Harold Leventhal Memorial Lecture at Columbia Law School and as the keynote lecture at the conference "Whither Democracy?" at Brandeis University; I am very grateful for the comments and suggestions offered on those occasions. I am also grateful to participants in workshops at the AEI-Brookings Joint Center for Regulatory Studies, Harvard Law School, the John F. Kennedy School of Government at Harvard University, the University of Chicago Law School, and Yale Law School.

Many friends and colleagues provided valuable comments and discussions, including Michael Abramowicz, Bruce

Ackerman, Ian Ayres, Jon Elster, Elizabeth Emens, Robert Hahn, Bernard Harcourt, Douglas Lichtman, Anup Malani, William Meadow, Martha Nussbaum, Eric Posner, Richard Posner, Adam Samaha, and Adrian Vermeule; Abramowicz and Samaha deserve extra thanks for rereading the manuscript when it was nearing completion. Exceptionally helpful readers' reports were produced by Jack Balkin, David Estlund, Robert MacCoun, and Richard Pildes, as well as by two anonymous reviewers.

When I was in the middle of the manuscript, I sent an e-mail to my friend and former colleague, Lawrence Lessig, asking him some naïve questions about information aggregation, wikis, and open source software. Lessig pointed me in extremely helpful directions; equally important, he invited me to post on his blog to try ideas and to receive comments from an extremely informed set of readers. This opportunity was exceptionally helpful, and I am most grateful to Lessig and to the numerous commenters for their thoughts, suggestions, and provocations. Though the book offers a mixed and highly ambivalent picture of blogs, my own experience chez Lessig was entirely positive. Lessig was also generous enough to offer a set of comments on the near-final manuscript.

At a later stage of the manuscript, I participated in a conference in Chicago, organized by Dan Drezner and Henry Farrell, titled "The Power and the Politics of Blogs." The participants made valuable corrections to several of my arguments, especially those in chapters 4 and 5. Thanks in particular to Drezner, Farrell, Eszter Hargittai, and Ethan Zuckerman. Special thanks to Zuckerman for generously reading relevant parts of the manuscript on wikis and open source software. Zuckerman's comments saved me from a number of errors and also added valuable information, with many extremely helpful contributions. Remaining mistakes are, of course, entirely my responsibility.

Warm thanks are due as well to two companies, Google and Microsoft. Like most authors, I owe a general debt to both companies for multiple services rendered; but in particular, I am grateful to experts there for their willingness to provide me with truly fascinating material about their internal prediction markets. Bo Cowgill at Google and Todd Proebsting at Microsoft deserve special gratitude for their generosity and help.

This book grows out of a more technical essay, "Group Judgments: Statistical Means, Deliberation, and Prediction Markets," *New York University Law Review* 80 (2005): 962. Although the book is significantly longer, and broadens and revises the argument quite substantially, I remain grateful to the editors of the *New York University Law Review* not only for permission to develop the argument presented there in book form, but also for numerous helpful suggestions. Wonderful research assistance was provided by Jeffrey Harris, Jessica Hertz, Ken Merber, and Robert Park. For financial support, I am grateful to the Herbert Fried Fund and to the Law and Economics Program at the University of Chicago Law School.

Particular thanks are due to three people. Reid Hastie provided a great deal of patient help and tutoring on group judgments. Saul Levmore taught me a lot about prediction markets and the Condorcet Jury Theorem. Dedi Felman, the book's editor, provided support and substantive help at multiple stages and made exceptionally helpful comments on the manuscript in the final weeks.

I dedicate the book to Leon Wieseltier. Leon and I became friends as students more than a quarter-century ago. At major and minor stages, across countless joys and some sadnesses, I have been lucky to benefit from his boundless generosity, humor, kindness, inventiveness, wisdom, independence of mind, sense, and sheer capacity for life.

Each member of society can have only a small fraction of the knowledge possessed by all, and . . . each is therefore ignorant of most of the facts on which the working of society rests. . . . civilization rests on the fact that we all benefit from knowledge which we do *not* possess. And one of the ways in which civilization helps us to overcome that limitation on the extent of individual knowledge is by conquering ignorance, not by the acquisition of more knowledge, but by the utilization of knowledge which is and which remains widely dispersed among individuals.

—Friedrich Hayek, *Law, Legislation, and Liberty*,
   vol. 1: *Rules and Order*

The presumption that Iraq had active WMD programs was so strong that formalized [intelligence community] mechanisms established to challenge assumptions and "group think," such as "red teams," "devil's advocacy," and other types of alternative or competitive analysis, were not utilized.

—Senate Select Committee on Intelligence, Report of the 108th
   Congress, *U.S. Intelligence Community's Prewar Intelligence
   Assessments on Iraq: Conclusions*

A very numerous assembly cannot be composed of very enlightened men. It is even probable than those comprising this assembly will on many matters combine great ignorance with many prejudices. . . . It follows that the more numerous the assembly, the more it will be exposed to the risk of making false decisions.

—Condorcet, *Selected Writings*

Imagine a world in which every single person is given free access to the sum of human knowledge. That's what we're doing.

—Jimmy Wales, Founder, Wikipedia

Contents /

Infotopia/

Introduction / **Dreams and Nightmares**

/ A Possible Future /

It is some time in the future. Businesses, governments, and individual lives have been fundamentally transformed, above all because of the rise of new methods for obtaining information. Collaborative projects, often involving numerous strangers, are growing in both scale and quality, to the benefit of millions of people. Many of these projects are open to every human being on the globe. It is also simple to find, almost instantly, the judgments of "people like you" about almost everything: books, movies, hotels, restaurants, vacation spots, museums, television programs, music, potential romantic partners, doctors, movie stars, and countless goods and services.

Some of the most dramatic changes involve public institutions. The United States continues to face a number of serious threats to its security, and the Department of Defense continues to play a central role in monitoring and counteracting those threats. But in crucial ways, the day-to-day operations of the department are strikingly different from what they were in the earliest years of the twenty-first century. Many of the department's internal documents are "wikis"—Web pages that are highly secure but that can be freely and immediately edited by anyone who has access to them. The department's personnel manual is a wiki, and new requirements and procedures can be instantly entered and made available to employees. Department of Defense lawyers have a wiki for critical legal issues, informally named Wikilaw and containing an extraordinary amount of material about legal problems of particular concern to the department. Some important files involving national security operate as wikis, too. These files are edited several times each day, as new information emerges. High-level officials in the department regularly consult the rapidly changing wikis involving North Korea, Iraq, and Iran.

Much of the department's work, of course, continues to involve predictions for a highly uncertain future: about the nature of apparent threats, about the stability of certain governments, about technology and even natural disasters. Department analysts frequently consult "prediction markets"—markets in which ordinary people are permitted to invest in, or bet on, what is likely to happen. In the past several years, the outcomes of prediction markets have proved exceedingly valuable to the department, helping it to predict accurately that an apparently unfriendly nation did not, in fact, have weapons of mass destruction.

The department has recently created an internal prediction market, allowing employees with relevant expertise to make "investments" in forecasts about issues on which the general public has little or no information. The early results of the department's market have been uncannily good. Recently the market accurately foresaw, as high-level officials did not, the fall of an unfriendly government in a Middle Eastern country.

Much of what is happening at the Department of Defense has close analogues throughout the private sector. All over the world, private organizations are relying on prediction markets to foresee the likely fates of their own products and services. Verizon, for example, takes full advantage of its internal prediction markets, which forecast sales, launch dates for new products, office openings, and much more. Warner Brothers and Dreamworks rely on such markets to project likely revenues from their films, sometimes even before production begins; company *planning is greatly influenced by these projections. Wikis are in pervasive use, allowing any authorized personnel in a company to edit important documents involving rapidly changing business plans. But many people believe that the most dramatic development is the growing movement toward "open source science."*

Through open source science, the patent system is avoided, and hence scientists do not need to pay for licenses to engage in various activities, such as transferring genes into plants and animals. As a result, free communication among scientists is much easier. According to one enthusiast, "It isn't about making it cost-free or busting patents. It's about harnessing the latent creativity of a very large number of people who are out of the loop right now."[1] Open source biotechnology has achieved international attention and even acclaim. "Opening the books on emerging technologies, making the information about how they work widely available and easily accessible, in turn creates the possibility of a global defense against accidents or the inevitable depredations of a few."[2]

/ True Stories /

All this is speculative fiction, with concocted accounts of the practices of the Department of Defense, Verizon, Warner Brothers, and Dreamworks. But the discussion of open source science is based on actual facts, and the quotations are entirely real. Even the speculative parts grow out of actual practices. With respect to the aggregation of information, we are in the midst of a genuine revolution—one that is simultaneously affecting businesses, governments, and individual lives all over the globe.

Consider just three examples:

1. How might a company forecast its own development? Google has tried an innovative method.[3] It created a

prediction market in which its employees could place "bets" about a variety of outcomes of importance to the company. Participants made forecasts about when products would launch, their likely success, and much more. They invested virtual money, which could be redeemed for various prizes. By and large, the outcomes of Google's prediction markets have been stunningly accurate. Dispersed knowledge within the company has been accurately aggregated in this way. The reason is that many employees, each with private information, have offered their own opinions, and the sum of those opinions is usually right.

2. In 2003, the American Civil Liberties Union received thousands of pages of documents relating to the treatment of detainees being held at Guantánamo Bay in Cuba. The ACLU was unable to review the documents simply because of the huge number of pages and the small number of people available to read them. But in 2005, a group of volunteers used wiki software to expedite the process; as a result, people can divide up their readings as they choose, and they can post their findings in a common space. The group was spurred into action by the influential liberal blog, Daily Kos. At the wiki called dKosopedia, volunteers have been reading and summarizing the massive material.

3. At a prominent university press, key judgments used to be made as a result of a deliberative process, in which editors discussed proposals with people from marketing and sales. But these processes did not do well in incorporating changes over time. Books are altered as they are written; costs change, too; and estimates of likely sales do not remain stable. The press now uses a special form, called "File 05," which operates as a wiki. The form is kept on a shared drive, with material that "anyone can edit." Updated material,

covering changes in the book or its prospects, is entered immediately. Individual knowledge is constantly reflected in the file, and the business is working better as a result.

/ A Problem and Some Solutions /

Information is widely dispersed in society. Most human beings on the planet have bits of information from which others might benefit. But groups and institutions often fail to obtain the information that individuals have. As a result, they end up making avoidable and sometimes disastrous mistakes.

Let us understand the word "group" to include any collection of people. So understood, a group might be a company, a religious organization, a legislature, a labor union, a college faculty, a student organization, a local government, even a nation. Suppose that the group's members, taken as a whole, already have a good deal of knowledge. How might groups elicit the information they need?

It is easy to identify four answers—four different methods of eliciting and aggregating information. First, groups might use the statistical average of the independent judgments of their members. Second, groups might attempt to improve on those independent judgments by using deliberation and asking for the reasoned exchange of facts, ideas, and opinions; perhaps members will vote, anonymously or otherwise, after deliberation has occurred. Third, groups might use the price system and develop some kind of market, through which group members, or those outside of the group, buy and sell on the basis of their judgments. Fourth, groups might enlist the Internet to obtain the information and perspectives of anyone who cares to participate. The Internet offers countless new possibilities here, encompassing the first three answers and going well beyond them. These possibilities include massive surveys, deliberative forums, prediction markets, books and resources that anyone can edit, and open participation combined with some kind of process for filtering and screening.

All of these methods have great potential, but all of them also run into serious difficulties. The underlying problems have implications not only for individual lives, and not only for private organizations, but also for many institutions involved in law and politics, including legislatures, administrative agencies, multimember courts, and even the White House and the Supreme Court. As we shall see, some of those problems might be reduced through careful institutional design—and through an understanding of how healthy aggregation of information can be made to occur.

For aggregating information, the Internet offers great risk as well as extraordinary promise. Both the risk and the promise come from the fact that with the Internet, it is easy to obtain the views and even the collaboration of hundreds, thousands, and conceivably even millions of people. Every day, like-minded people can and do sort themselves into echo chambers of their own design, leading to wild errors, undue confidence, and unjustified extremism. But every day, the Internet also offers exceedingly valuable exercises in information aggregation, as people learn a great deal from the dispersed bits of information that other people have. Many people are curious, and they often seek out perspectives that run counter to their own.

As a result, there are remarkable exercises in the development of cumulative knowledge, producing an astonishing range of new goods and activities. We shall see that some of the underlying methods are novel and exceedingly dramatic. They will be used far more ambitiously than they now are.

With respect to the aggregation of information, we are in the first stages of a revolution.

/ Information Cocoons and Wikis /

In the early days of the Internet, Nicholas Negroponte, a media and technology specialist at the Massachusetts Institite of Technology, prophecied the emergence of "the Daily Me," an entirely personalized newspaper in which each of us could select topics and perspectives that we like.[4] The Daily Me is a genuine opportunity, or risk, for some of us, with occasionally unfortunate consequences for business and democracy alike. The central problem involves *information cocoons*: communications universes in which we hear only what we choose and only what comforts and pleases us.

If a company creates an information cocoon, it is unlikely to prosper, for its own decisions will not be adequately challenged from the inside. Some companies fail for this reason. If members of a political group—or a nation's leaders—live in a cocoon, they are unlikely to think well, simply because their own preconceptions will become entrenched. Some nations run into disaster for this reason. It can be comforting for leaders and others to live in information cocoons—warm, friendly places where everyone shares our views—but major errors are the price of our comfort. For private and public institutions, cocoons can turn into terrible nightmares.

But there is another side of the story. Might human knowledge be seen as a wiki? Certainly what we know accumulates over time, as each person obtains access to information held by widely diverse others and also contributes to that information. In the recent past, this development of cumulative knowledge has become much faster and much easier. Begin with products and services: In just a few seconds, it is already easy to find what "we" know and think about cars, restaurants, movies, books, and services. In a few seconds more, it is simple to add to this collective knowledge, some of which may turn out to be anything but comfortable. (You might learn that the car you think you love needs a lot of maintenance, or smells funny.) On the Internet, information is being shared at an astounding rate. Amazon.com, for example, aggregates information both through its ranking system and through customer reviews, which can be both helpful and numerous. Often people are surprised by what they see. Other examples are growing, in number and in quality, every day, even every minute. The great advantage of aggregated information is that, most of the time, it is stunningly accurate.

What is true of products and services is true of politics, science, literature, and much more. Suppose you would like to learn about topics about which you now know nothing, or that you are interested in exploring new or opposing points of view. You can satisfy your curiosity almost instantly. Often you will be challenged—sadder, in a way, but also wiser. A great deal of material, both technical and more general, can be found on multiple wikis, involving Irish politics, flu, language, *Star Wars*, and far more; and if the material is incomplete or incorrect, anyone can add new material or correct it at the touch of a button.

No one writes a wiki. We all do, and for that reason a wiki can be a collective product, sometimes even a Daily Us. Whether or not you have ever contributed to a wiki or a prediction market, many of your fellow citizens are doing so, and their contributions are producing cumulative, aggregated information that affects both private and public behavior. Some company executives, formerly living in cocoons, have been surprised and illuminated by what wikis and prediction markets have to say.

In these and other ways, the Daily Us, involving the rapid growth of cumulative knowledge, is not a prediction. To an increasing degree, we are living in it.

/ Deliberation, Democracy, and "Particles of Reason" /

Most of the time, both private and public institutions prefer to make decisions through some form of deliberation. Building on this fact, many people have paid a great deal of attention to deliberative accounts of democracy itself. Like many other nations, the United States aspires to be a deliberative democracy, in part on the ground that with deliberation, officials can consider diverse perspectives and a great deal of information.

The theoretical foundations of deliberative democracy have been elaborated in much detail, most prominently by the German philosopher Jürgen Habermas.[5] Indeed, increasing attention is being devoted to methods for making democratic processes more deliberative. Perhaps a more deliberative nation can avoid serious mistakes both in war and in peace. Carl Schmitt, critic as well as theorist of democracy, wrote, "Parliament is . . . the place in which particles of reason that are strewn unequally among human beings gather themselves and bring public power under their control."[6] If our goal is to have access to multiple "particles of reason," deliberation may be the best path. Because so many people are inclined to this view,[7] I devote a great deal of attention to it here and attempt to show that it suffers from extremely serious flaws.

James Fishkin, for example, has pioneered the idea of the "deliberative poll," by which people are asked to deliberate together on public issues and to state their judgments only after the deliberative process is complete.[8] Fishkin and Bruce Ackerman have gone so far as to suggest a new national holiday, Deliberation Day, on which people are asked to congregate in groups to discuss and debate important issues of public policy.[9] Perhaps the proposal is unrealistic. Perhaps citizens as a whole should not be expected to deliberate much in a free society. But even if most people cannot spend a lot of time on deliberation, representatives are supposed to do precisely that.

A key question is this: Does deliberation actually lead to better decisions? Often it does not.[10] Group members may impose pressures on one another, leading to extremism or to a consensus on falsehood rather than truth. The idea of "groupthink," coined by Irving Janis, suggests that groups may well promote unthinking uniformity and dangerous self-censorship, thus failing to combine information and enlarge the range of arguments.[11] Countless groups do badly not in spite of deliberation but because of it. The problem is that deliberating groups often do not obtain the knowledge that their members actually have.

As a real-world example of a serious failure of deliberation, consider the account in the 2004 report of the Senate Select Committee on Intelligence. That report explicitly accused the Central Intelligence Agency of groupthink, through which the agency's predisposition to find a serious threat from Iraq caused it to fail to explore alternative possibilities and to obtain and use the information that its employees held.[12] In the committee's view, the CIA "demonstrated several aspects of group think: examining few alternatives, selective gathering of information, pressure to conform within the group or withhold criticism, and collective rationalization."[13] The agency showed a "tendency to reject information that contradicted the presumption" that Iraq had weapons of mass destruction. Because of that presumption, the agency failed to use its own formalized methods "to challenge assumptions and 'group think,' such as 'red teams,' 'devil's advocacy,' and other types of alternative or competitive analysis." Above all, the committee's conclusions emphasize the CIA's failure to elicit and aggregate information that was actually in the possession of its employees.

This claim is a remarkable and even uncanny echo of one that followed the 2003 investigation of failures at NASA surrounding the explosion of the space shuttle *Columbia*. The investigation revealed the agency's similar failure to elicit competing views, including those based on information held by agency employees.[14] The Columbia Accident Investigation Board explicitly attributed the accident to NASA's unfortunate culture, one that does too little to elicit information. In the board's words, NASA lacks "checks and balances." It pressures people to follow a "party line." At NASA, "it is difficult for minority and dissenting opinions to percolate up through the agency's hierarchy," even though, the board contended, effective safety programs require the encouragement of minority opinions and a willingness to acknowledge, rather than to conceal, bad news.[15] The general lesson is that political leaders, even at the highest levels, often live in cocoons, and deliberation provides far less help than it should.

To explain the failures of deliberation and the promise of other methods for aggregating information, I explore the consequences of two forces. The first consists of *informational influences*, which cause group members to fail to disclose what they know out of respect for the information publicly announced by others. If many people seem to think that Iraq possesses weapons of mass destruction, or that a proposed shuttle launch is safe, then others might be quiet, thinking: How can many people be wrong? The second force involves *social pressures*, which lead people to silence themselves to avoid the disapproval of peers and supervisors. Even if you believe that group members are blundering, you might not say a word simply because you do not want to risk their displeasure.

As a result of these two forces, groups often fall prey to a series of problems. They do not correct but instead amplify individual errors. They emphasize information held by all or most at the expense of information held by a few or one. They fall victim to bandwagon or cascade effects. They end up in a more extreme position in line with the predeliberation tendencies of their members. Even federal judges, specialists in the law, are vulnerable to the relevant pressures. Both Republican and Democratic appointees to the federal courts show especially ideological voting patterns when they are sitting with other judges appointed by presidents of the same political party.[16] Indeed, deliberation often fails to aggregate information even as it increases agreement and confidence among group members. A confident, cohesive, error-prone group—a company, a labor union, a military unit, a nation— is nothing to celebrate. On the contrary, it might be extremely dangerous both to itself and to others.

/ Beyond Deliberation /

How might these dangers be avoided? How might we obtain access to the knowledge that is held by many minds?

One possibility is to build on the price system. As emphasized by socialism's greatest critic, Friedrich Hayek, the price system is a "marvel," simply because of its extraordinary power to aggregate information. As Hayek saw, markets produce prices for steel, books, coffee, and candy in a way that incorporates the dispersed information held by numerous people. In markets, people have an extremely strong incentive to get it right. Certain information may remain "hidden" in deliberating groups, but if there is profit to be had, consumers and investors will act on that information, which will not remain hidden for long. Partly for that reason, market prices typically reflect a massive amount of accurate information. They even create a kind of Daily Us.

Hayek did have an important blind spot. Markets can incorporate falsehood as well as truth. Fads and fashions can ensure inflated prices. A great deal of recent evidence shows that markets are subject to the very problems that infect deliberation—not only for ordinary products, but also for stocks and cars and real estate. We shall nonetheless see that prediction markets, a new innovation, often do startlingly well simply because they are so effective at pooling information. Who will win the next election or the Academy Award for best actress? What products will make money, and what products are bound to fail? Will the economy of Saudi Arabia prosper in the next year? Through prediction markets, people can "invest" in the probability that certain events will occur, and they will gain or lose money as a result. The resulting forecasts incorporate, and provide, a lot of knowledge. They are being enlisted by prominent businesses; governments would do well to use them, too.

What is the best way to ensure innovation? Open source software also pools the information and even the creativity of numerous people—not always because of economic incentives, but sometimes because people like to contribute to improvements. In a slogan made famous by Eric Raymond, an open source theorist, "Given enough eyeballs, all bugs are shallow."[17] The idea of open source is hardly limited to software. Open source products, including biotechnology and medicine, might ultimately end up saving numerous lives, especially, but not only, in poor countries.

The same principle helps account for the success of Wikipedia, the free online encyclopedia that can be edited by anyone at all. Indeed, wikis of various sorts are cropping up all over the Internet, and they often work well as devices for aggregating dispersed information. The rise of blogs, enabling ordinary people to reach a significant audience, might well be celebrated as a way of ensuring that far more bits of information enter the public domain. Unfortunately, blogs spread errors and falsehood as well, especially when like-minded people are mostly talking and listening to one another.

To keep the analysis simple, I focus not on controversial judgments of value but on questions with demonstrably correct answers, now or in the future. What exactly happened in World War II? Does a certain nation have nuclear weapons? Will a human being be cloned? Will the government of Saudi Arabia be toppled? Will there be a flu pandemic? Will a terrorist attack hit the United States in the next year? An understanding of how we might find, and fail to find, answers to such questions should have implications for questions of value as well. If deliberation often fails to produce good answers to simple questions of fact, then it is also likely to fail to produce good answers to disputed issues of value. As it happens, the problems posed by informational pressure and social influences apply in all domains. They infect our most fundamental judgments about morality and policy, not merely judgments about facts.

/ The Plan /

This book consists of six chapters, exploring different methods for obtaining access to many minds. Chapter 1 begins the analysis with a description of a simple method for aggregating privately held information, one that relies on majority rule. Certain questions might be answered by asking a large group of people and assuming that the majority's answer, or the average answer, is right. The resulting judgments of these "statistical groups" can be remarkably accurate.[18] If we have access to many minds, we might trust the average response, a point that bears on the foundations of democracy itself. But accuracy is likely only under identifiable conditions, in which people do not suffer from a systematic bias that makes their answers worse than random. If we asked everyone in the world to estimate the population of Egypt, or to say how many people have served on the U.S. Supreme Court, or to guess the distance between Mars and Venus, the average answer is likely to be wildly off.

Chapters 2 and 3 turn to deliberation. I explain why it is both tempting and reasonable to expect that deliberation will lead to major improvements on the judgments of statistical groups. Many people have expressed the hope that deliberation can ensure the triumph of the "forceless force of the better argument."[19] Unfortunately, the hope is often dashed. Informational pressures and social influences contribute to the amplification of errors, hidden profiles, cascade effects, and group polarization. Large groups are often no better than small ones on this count.

Chapter 4 turns to some exciting and largely novel methods for aggregating information. I compare the price system and prediction markets, in which many people invest in the outcomes of events. The foundation of the discussion is Hayek's treatment of the price system and his emphasis on its remarkable ability to adapt itself "to millions of facts which in their entirely are not known to anybody."[20] We shall see that despite its excessive sunniness, this argument contains some profound truth. In particular, prediction markets have performed remarkably well in diverse settings, by, for example, calling presidential elections with uncanny accuracy and also predicting the major Oscar winners, changes in the economy, and even the weather. But markets are not free from the problems that infect deliberation. The task is to identify the circumstances in which prediction markets will work well.

Chapter 5 turns to three ways to use the Internet to obtain access to many minds: wikis, open source software, and blogs. Wikis allow anyone to make changes in text. They typically lack layers of review, and so there is a risk that vandals, or people who are simply wrong, will defeat the enterprise. Nonetheless, some wikis, most notably Wikipedia, have been a smashing success, and there is much to learn from this process. It is an understatement to say that much more can be done with the wiki form. And as we shall see, much of the excitement of the open source movement stems from a simple fact: If we understand why open source software works well, we might be able to use the open source idea in many other contexts, including medicine and science. These various points bear on other efforts to obtain the views of many minds, as, for example, in the aggregation of reviewers' judgments about movies and art, and the use of customer feedback on eBay and Amazon.com.

Many people are celebrating blogs as a way of ensuring that dispersed information comes to public light; it is true that the mass media itself has been corrected, on prominent occasions, by bloggers. But blogs do not produce a price, a product, or a text. In fact, the blogosphere offers a cacophony of sounds, and in terms of accuracy and quality, there is endless diversity—not merely clarity and sense and justified outrage, but also half-truths, falsehoods, confusions, self-promotion, and lies. In many ways, this is a blessing, because so much information is able to emerge, but all of the problems with deliberation can be found there.

Chapter 6 offers an evaluation and comparison of various ways of eliciting and aggregating knowledge. In addition, I investigate ways to improve deliberation by both private and public groups. The key question is how to obtain dispersed information, and what we learn from prediction markets, wikis, and open source software offers many clues about how to do exactly that. Much of the book emphasizes the pervasive problems with deliberation. But the ultimate goal is to mend it, not to end it.

As I emphasize throughout, efforts to aggregate information can lead people to extremism,[21] complacency, and error. Some people do live in information cocoons, spending much of their time immersed in their particular Daily Me. But many other people are taking advantage of new methods for uncovering the widely dispersed knowledge that people actually have. Some of America's largest companies have used wikis and prediction markets to excellent effect. The most successful governments tenaciously guard against the procedural problems described at the CIA and NASA; they ensure that dispersed information is elicited rather than hidden. As we shall also see, prediction markets, wikis, and open source software offer new ways of accomplishing that goal—and they simultaneously help to show how to make the old ways work much better.

Chapter One / **The (Occasional) Power of Numbers**

Suppose that we want to answer a disputed question of fact. The question might involve past events: When was Calvin Coolidge elected president? How tall is the Eiffel Tower? How many home runs did Babe Ruth hit? Or the issue might involve a prediction about the future: Will Iran or North Korea pose a genuine threat to U.S. security? Is global warming a serious problem? Will the poverty rate, or concentrations of specified air pollutants, increase in the next year? Will a particular product sell? What will be the effect of a hurricane? Is a flu pandemic going to strike Europe? Will an endangered species recover?

A great deal of evidence suggests that under certain conditions, a promising way to answer such questions is this: *Ask a large number of people and take the average answer.* As emphasized by James Surowiecki in his engaging and illuminating *The Wisdom of Crowds*, large groups can, in a sense, be wiser than experts.[1] When the relevant conditions are met, the average answer, which we might describe as the group's "statistical answer," is often accurate, where accuracy is measured by reference to objectively demonstrable facts.

Here's one example: In 2004, members of the Society for American Baseball Research were asked to predict the winners of the baseball playoffs.[2] Remarkably, strong majorities of the 413 respondents correctly predicted all of the first-round winners: New York, Boston, Houston, and

St. Louis. At least as remarkably, a majority predicted, correctly, that St. Louis would win the National League pennant, and a large plurality predicted that the Red Sox would win the American League pennant. A plurality also favored the Red Sox to win the World Series. Hence, the favored choice of the group was right 100 percent of the time.

Here's another example: In 1999, the world champion of chess, Garry Kasparov, agreed to play against the entire world. The game was played on the Internet, with the World Team's decisions coming as a result of majority or plurality vote. Four young chess experts were asked to suggest possible moves, but the world was entitled to do as it wished. To promote extended thinking, moves were slowed down to permit one move every two days. Before the game began, it was widely expected that Kasparov would win easily. How could the majority or plurality view of the world's players, almost none anywhere near Kasparov's level, hope to compete with the world's champion? But the game turned out to be exceptionally close. After four grueling months, Kasparov ultimately prevailed. But he acknowledged that he had never expended as much effort on any game in his life, and he declared that this was the "greatest game in the history of chess."[3]

One final example: To know whether a new movie is good, it is useful to consult the judgment of the reviewer for the local newspaper, especially if the reviewer is someone whose opinions you know and trust. But for many people, it is far more useful to aggregate the views of a number of reviewers, and to take the average view as the most informative. Indeed, several magazines and newspapers now report not merely the reaction of their own critic, but also the aggregated judgments of numerous critics, showing a clear awareness of the value of the average view of many people.

Rotten Tomatoes, a Web site, makes it a general practice to aggregate the evaluations of movie reviewers.

It is well-known that statistical answers from groups of sufficiently large sizes tend to match the views of population-wide samples. If you ask one hundred randomly selected people to name their favorite television shows, you might well end up with a good sense of the nation's favorite televison shows. This finding helps to explain why presidential polls tend to do fairly well: A randomly selected sample will mirror the views of the population as a whole. The same point helps to explain the use of juries as a measure of community sentiment.[4] If twelve randomly selected people come to a certain conclusion, there is good reason to think that the community as a whole would come to the same conclusion. Through the same route, we can understand the remarkable success of Google, the search engine. Why is Google so good at finding what a particular searcher wants? The answer is that it knows what *most* searchers want, and most people want what most people want.[5]

But here the question is what is true, not what populations think. Let us therefore explore how statistical groups actually perform.

/ Evidence /

Many of the studies of statistical groups involve quantitative estimates. Consider a few examples:

1. In an early study, Hazel Knight asked college students to estimate the temperature of a classroom.[6] Individual judgments ranged from 60 degrees to 85 degrees; the statistical judgment of the group was 72.4 degrees, very close to the actual temperature of 72 degrees. That judgment was better than 80 percent of the individual judgments.

2. When people are judging the numbers of beans in a jar, the group average is almost always better than the individual judgments of the vast majority of members. In one such experiment, a group of fifty-six students was asked about a jar containing 850 beans; the group estimate was 871, a better guess than that of all but one of the students.[7]

3. Asked to rank the sizes of ten piles of buckshot, each only slightly different in size from the others, the combined group's average guess was 94.5 percent accurate, far more so than that of almost all individual group members.[8]

4. The British scientist Francis Galton sought to draw lessons about collective intelligence by examining a competition in which contestants attempted to judge the weight of a fat ox at a regional fair in England. The ox weighed 1,198 pounds; the average guess, from the 787 contestants, was 1,197 pounds.[9]

In light of these findings, many questions might be answered, not deliberatively, and not with markets or economic incentives, but simply by consulting many minds and selecting the average response. Imagine that a large company is attempting to project its sales for certain products in the following year; perhaps the company needs an accurate projection to know how much to spend on labor and promotion. Might it do best to poll its salespeople and trust the average number?[10] Or suppose that a company is deciding whether to hire a new employee. Should it rely, not on deliberation, but on the average view of its relevant personnel? (Should people answer questions about their personal lives—where to live, what car to buy, what job to take, whom to date, whom to marry—by asking a number of people and taking the average answer?)

Or turn to the political domain and suppose that the question is whether a war effort, or an environmental initiative, will go well by some identifiable standard. Should the president poll his advisors and take the average answer? More broadly, might democratic judgments be almost always right simply because many people are being asked their views? To answer these questions, we have to know why, in the relevant studies, the average judgment is so accurate.

/ The Condorcet Jury Theorem /

The accuracy of judgments of statistical groups is best explained by reference to the Condorcet Jury Theorem, which offers one of the most interesting results in modern social theory.[11] To see how the Jury Theorem works, suppose that people are answering the same question with two possible answers, one false and one true. Assume, too, that the probability that each voter will answer correctly exceeds 50 percent. The Jury Theorem says that the probability of a correct answer by a majority of the group increases toward 100 percent as the size of the group increases. The key point is that groups will do better than individuals, and big groups better than little ones, so long as two conditions are met: Majority rule is used, and each person is more likely than not to be correct.

The theorem is based on some fairly simple arithmetic. Suppose, for example, that there is a three-person group in which each member has a 67 percent probability of being right. The probability that a majority vote will produce the correct answer is 74 percent.[12] As the size of the group increases, this probability increases, too. It should be clear that as the likelihood of a correct answer by individual members increases, the likelihood of a correct answer by the group also increases, at least if majority rule is used. If group members are 80 percent likely to be right individually, and if the group contains ten or more people, the probability of a correct answer by the majority is overwhelmingly high—very close to 100 percent.

Consider in this regard the hugely popular Zagat Survey, which uses consumers' evaluations as the basis for convenient and well-organized guides to dining, travel, and leisure. In the words of the Zagat Web site, its services enable you to "see how thousands of people like you rate over 30,000 Restaurants, Nightspots, Hotels and Attractions." There are Zagat restaurant guides for more than seventy markets worldwide, as well as guides to hotels, resorts, and airlines. The premise of the Zagat Survey, as stated by the Zagats themselves, is that "rating a restaurant on the basis of thousands of experiences [is] inherently more accurate than relying on one reviewer."[13] Zagat provides all sorts of evaluations on its Web site, including "out-takes." (Examples: "Makes hunger an attractive alternative"; "To call the food blech is an insult to blech"; "The food fills you up—if you can keep it down.") The phenomenal success of the Zagat Survey is a tribute to the Condorcet Jury Theorem. Because of the large numbers of people involved, and because their own judgments are (mostly) better than random, the likelihood of an accurate evaluation is very high.

Notwithstanding its simplicity, the Jury Theorem has implications for all sorts of questions, including the justification of democracy itself.[14] Its importance lies in its demonstration that groups are likely to do better than individuals, and large groups better than small ones, *if* majority rule is used and *if* each person is more likely than not to be correct. The point bears on decisions of all kinds of groups, including businesses, religious organizations, even political institutions. Suppose, for example, that employees at a large sneaker company are asked how many pairs of a new brand are likely to sell in the next year. If the employees are better-than-random guessers, and if there are a lot of them, the average answer will probably be fairly accurate. Or suppose that doctors in a particular hospital are asked whether a particular operation is likely to be successful. If the doctors have relevant expertise, and if there are more than a few doctors, the average answer may well turn out to be the right one.

If we shift the lens from voters to representatives, we can appreciate the argument for a large legislative body, such as the U.S. House of Representatives; if each representative is more likely than not to be right, then the majority is highly likely to be right.[15] Perhaps the outcomes of democratic processes will generally be sound simply because majority rule is used and because most citizens are more likely to be right than wrong.[16] For this reason, the Jury Theorem might be taken to support democracy itself.

In fact, the Jury Theorem is easily taken to provide a new reason to respect the often ridiculed outcomes of standard opinion polls. Under the stated conditions, the majority view can be trusted. If people are asked their beliefs about some question, including the probability of some future event, the answer might be far better than a random guess, at least if most people are responding with something even a little better than a random guess.

In the context of statistical groups, several of Condorcet's stringent and somewhat unrealistic assumptions are met. Indeed, the likelihood that they will be met is higher with statistical groups than with deliberating ones. Condorcet assumed that (1) people would be unaffected by whether their votes would be decisive, (2) people would not be affected by one another's votes, and (3) the probability that one group member would be right would be statistically unrelated to the probability that another group member would be right.[17] The first two assumptions plainly hold for statistical groups, such as those assessing the number of beans in a jar or the weight of animals. People do not know what others are guessing, and hence they cannot be influenced by a belief that their judgments will make the difference to that of the group. The third assumption may or may not be violated. Those who have similar training, or who work closely together, will be likely to see things in the same way, possibly leading to a violation of the third assumption. On the other hand, the Condorcet Jury Theorem has been shown to work even in the face of violations of this third assumption;[18] I put the technical complexities to one side here.[19]

The Dark Side of the Jury Theorem /

There is a dark side to the Jury Theorem, and it, too, has important implications. Suppose that each individual in a group is more likely to be wrong than right. If so, the likelihood that the group's majority will decide correctly falls to *zero* as the size of the group increases!

Imagine that an organization consists of a number of people, each of whom is at least 51 percent likely to be mistaken. The organization might be a political party, a religious group, a university faculty, or a terrorist group. The probability that the organization will err approaches 100 percent as the size of the group expands. Condorcet explicitly signaled this possibility and its source: "In effect, when the probability of the truth of a voter's opinion falls below ½, there must be a reason why he decides less well than one would at random. The reason can only be found in the prejudices to which this voter is subject."[20] The errors might stem not only from "prejudices," but also from confusion and incompetence. On tricky math problems, there is no reason to think that the average answer of a large group will be right. So, too, on complex issues involving politics. Even if people are competent, they might well be led astray, especially if they are subject to "prejudices" or if they are dealing with highly technical questions.

Of course, falsehoods are often the conventional wisdom. We could imagine a bizarre version of Zagat Surveys, consisting of people who do not know how to evaluate restaurants; the resulting information would be unhelpful. In many contexts, large numbers of people are in fact likely to blunder. "Many Germans believe that drinking water after eating cherries is deadly; they also believe that putting ice in soft drinks is unhealthy. The English, however, rather enjoy a cold drink of water after some cherries; and Americans love icy refreshments."[21] At least one large group must be wrong (the Germans, I believe!). A less innocuous example: In some nations, strong majorities believe that Arab terrorists were not responsible for the attacks of September 11, 2001. According to the Pew Research Institute, 93 percent of Americans believe that Arab terrorists destroyed the World Trade Center, whereas only 11 percent of Kuwaitis believe that Arab terrorists destroyed the World Trade Center.[22] (And the citizens of Kuwait, saved from Saddam Hussein by the United States, might be expected to agree with Americans on this issue.)

In short, the optimistic conclusion of the Jury Theorem holds only if we assume a certain level of accuracy on the part of the people involved. For many reasons, the level of accuracy may turn out to be low.

/ Fun with Numbers /

To get a clearer sense of why statistical groups often perform so well, note that even if everyone in the group is not more than 50 percent likely to be right, the theorem's predictions may well continue to hold. Suppose, for example, that 60 percent of people are 51 percent likely to be right and that 40 percent of people are 50 percent likely to be right; or that 45 percent of people are 40 percent likely to be right and 55 percent of people are 65 percent likely to be right; or even that 51 percent of people are 51 percent likely to be right and 49 percent of people are merely 50 percent likely to be right. Even under these conditions, the likelihood of a correct answer, via majority vote, will move toward 100 percent as the size of the group increases. It will not move as quickly as it would if every group member were highly likely to be right, but it will nonetheless move.

We could imagine endless variations on these numbers. The point is that even if a significant number of group members are more likely to be wrong than right, majority vote can produce the correct answer if the group is big enough. Consider another possibility, one with great practical importance: 40 percent of the group are more likely than not to be right, and 60 percent are only 50 percent likely to be right, but the errors of the 60 percent are *entirely random*. Because those who blunder do so randomly, the group, if it is large enough, will still end up with the right answer. Here is the reason: If a core of people has some insight into what's right, and if the rest of the group makes genuinely random errors, the majority will be driven in the direction set by the core. Suppose that one thousand people are asked the name of the actress who played Princess Leia in the first *Star Wars* trilogy and are given two possible answers: Carrie Fisher or Meryl Streep. If 40 percent of the group choose Carrie Fisher (the right answer, of course!), and if the other 60 percent make random guesses, Carrie Fisher will emerge with the highest number of votes.

Of course, most of the relevant judgments in studies of statistical groups do not involve a binary choice, that is, a choice between two possibilities. The easiest cases for the Jury Theorem ask a simple yes/no question, or one in which the right answer to a quantitative problem is one hundred or one thousand. Compare the very different question of how many beans are in a jar, how many pounds a given object weighs, how many bombs a nation has, or how many copies of a certain book will sell in the following year. When many options are offered, will the Jury Theorem hold? Note first that in answering such questions, each person is effectively being asked to answer a long series of binary questions: ten beans or a thousand beans, twenty beans or five hundred beans, fifty beans or one hundred beans, and so on. If a sufficiently large group is asked to answer such questions, and if most individual answers will be better than random, the average answer may well turn out to be highly accurate.

Unfortunately, the combination of probabilities for a series of binary results might mean that things will turn out poorly. If someone is 51 percent likely to answer each of two questions correctly, the probability that he or she will answer both questions correctly is only slightly higher than 25 percent. Suppose that you are 51 percent likely to be right on whether there are 800 or 780 beans in a jar, and also 51 percent likely to be right on whether there are 780 or 760 beans in a jar. Sad to say, you're almost 75 percent likely to get one or both of the two questions wrong; and things get rapidly worse as the number of questions increases. If someone is 51 percent likely to answer each of five questions correctly, the likelihood that he or she will answer all five questions correctly is very small: a little over 3 percent. But with many large groups, the average answer will nonetheless be quite accurate. Here is the key point: If a significant number of people are more likely to choose the correct answer than any of the incorrect ones, and if errors are randomly distributed, then the average judgment will be quite reliable. The reason is that the errors will be randomly assigned to the various possibilities, and the right answer will emerge as the most popular.

More technical analysis demonstrates that even with a range of options, the correct outcome is more likely to attract plurality support than any of the others.[23] The central idea is that if voters face three or more choices, the likelihood that the best option will win a plurality increases with the size of the group *if* each individual voter is more likely to vote for the best option than for any of the other ones.[24] As the number of voters expands to infinity, the likelihood that the correct answer will be the plurality's choice increases to 100 percent.

To bring the theory down to earth, consider the television show *Who Wants to Be a Millionaire?* In this show, contestants, when stumped, are permitted to pose questions of fact to a personally appointed "expert" (someone thought by the contestant to know a great deal) or, instead, the studio audience. The studio audience significantly outperforms the expert. Indeed, the studio answers are strikingly accurate, with the plurality proving to be right more than 90 percent of the time.[25] The Condorcet Jury Theorem helps explain why this is so. The guesses of most audience members are better than random. And when most members of the audience do not know the answer, their guesses tend to be randomly distributed, and hence those who know the right answer can produce an accurate winner by plurality vote.

But now return to the dark side of the Jury Theorem, and consider a situation in which the answers of 51 percent of the group are likely to be *worse* than random. In that situation, the likelihood that the majority of the group will err increases toward 100 percent as the size of the group increases. The same problem can beset pluralities, if the plurality is more likely than not to err and if the judgments of those outside the plurality are random. Under those unhappy circumstances, the likelihood of a mistake will move toward 100 percent as the size of the group expands.

The numbers are artificial, but the problem is all too real. For the number of beans in a jar, or the weight of an ox, or the particular questions asked on *Who Wants to Be a Millionaire?*, people are not wholly at sea. But if audience members were asked to answer some technical question—the weight of the moon, the distance from Mars to Venus, the number of people who have served on the U.S. Supreme Court—there is no reason to think the plurality would be right.

/ Blunders /

In this light, we can identify two situations in which the judgment of a statistical group will be wrong. The first are those in which group members show a systematic bias. The second, a generalization of the first, are those in which their answers are worse than random. The failures of statistical judgments in these circumstances have strong implications for other social failures as well—as individual blunders, with respect to actual or likely facts, are transformed into blunders by private and public institutions. Often statistical groups will be wrong. Sometimes they will be disastrously wrong.

Bias /

A systematic bias in one or another direction will create serious problems for the group's answers. Suppose that a large number of Nazis were asked to answer some question about the practices of Jews, or that thousands of slaveholders were asked to assess the intellectual capacities of slaves, or that Arab terrorists were asked about the recent history of the United States, or that men with discriminatory attitudes were asked to make some evaluations of women's abilities. Major errors would be inevitable, however large the number of people involved. Or suppose that some bias is leading people to favor one or another product (say, shoes or cereal) or even a candidate for public office; perhaps most citizens have been manipulated or misled. The dark side of the Jury Theorem can guarantee error from many minds. Condorcet was fully alert to this problem, saying that it is "necessary, furthermore, that voters be enlightened; and that they be the more enlightened, the more complicated the question upon which they decide."[26]

Consider a simple example. It is well-known that people are susceptible to *anchors*, in the form of starting points that can greatly bias their judgments. If, for example, an experimenter anchors people on a misleading number, the average judgment will almost certainly be wrong. Suppose that a jar contains eight hundred jelly beans, and the experimenter happens to say, sweetly and very quietly, "Many jars of jelly beans, though not necessarily this one, have five hundred jelly beans," or even, "I'm asking this question to 250 people."[27] In either case, the low number will likely operate as an anchor, and people's answers will be systematically biased toward understating the actual number, producing an unreliable average. One study demonstrates more generally that a group's statistical estimate is likely to be erroneous "when the material is unfamiliar, distorted in a way such that all individuals are prone to make similar errors of estimation."[28]

The Jury Theorem is about juries, of course, and anchors have significant effects all over the legal system. For example, the plaintiff's initial request is likely to affect the jury's damage awards for harms that are difficult to monetize. Suppose that someone is suing for libel, sexual harassment, or emotional distress, and that he seeks $75 million in damages. That (perhaps outlandishly high) number is likely to influence the jury simply because it operates as an anchor. Groups are no less subject to those effects than individuals.[29] Even judges have been found to be subject to irrelevant anchors,[30] and there is every reason to believe that multi-member courts would be at least as vulnerable to them as individual judges are.[31]

The effect of anchors is a simple demonstration that when many people suffer from the same bias, the average answer will not be reliable at all. Legislatures and executive officers may make bad decisions for this very reason. Speaking of democracy in general, Condorcet made the point clearly, calling it "a rather important observation": "A very numerous assembly cannot be composed of very enlightened men. It is even probable than those comprising this assembly will on many matters combine great ignorance with many prejudices. Thus there will be a great number of questions on which the probability of the truth of each voter will be below ½. It follows that the more numerous the assembly, the more it will be exposed to the risk of making false decisions."[32] (It is often hoped that deliberation will correct people's mistakes, a hope to which I will turn in due course.)

Condorcet contended that because of the risk of pervasive prejudice and ignorance, "it is clear that it can be dangerous to give a democratic constitution to an unenlightened people." Even in societies with relatively enlightened people, he believed, citizens should not make decisions themselves, but should generally be restricted to the role of electing representatives, "those whose opinions will have a large enough probability of being true."[33] There is a clear and direct link between Condorcet's conclusions on this count and the founding of the U.S. Constitution. The American founders, most prominently James Madison, did not want direct self-rule, preferring instead to permit voters to choose enlightened and virtuous representatives. The U.S. Constitution is based on a belief that ordinary citizens, fallible as they are, should not make laws on their own. Their role is instead to select lawmakers: enlightened people "whose opinions will have a large enough probability of being true."

Random or Worse /

Suppose that people are asked not about the number of jelly beans in a jar, but about the number of atoms in a jelly bean. On that question, most people's answers are hopelessly ill-informed, and there is no reason at all to trust their judgments. If every person in the world were asked to guess the number of atoms in a jelly bean, the average answer is most unlikely to be accurate. If every person in France were asked to specify the gross domestic product of India, or the number of World Series won by the New York Yankees, or the total population of Ethiopia, the average answer would probably be wildly off.

Consider the embarrassing outcome of a small-scale study that I conducted at my home institution, the University of Chicago Law School. A number of faculty members were asked the weight, in pounds, of the fuel that powers space shuttles. The actual answer is 4 million pounds. The median response was two hundred thousand; the average was 55,790,555 (because of one outlier choice)—both wildly inaccurate.

In a binary choice, of course, people's answers will be worse than random only if they are unaware of how little they know. If they know that they are likely to be wrong, they should choose randomly, which gives them a 50 percent probability of being right. But sometimes people think they know a lot more than they do, and many tasks do not involve binary choices at all. We have seen that when there are many options, a plurality can do well *if* group members are more likely to choose the right option than any of the wrong ones. But even so, there is a qualification: The right option will attract fewer votes than all the wrong ones if these are taken in combination. Suppose, for example, that Americans are asked the name of the president at the time Congress enacted the Occupational Safety and Health Act and are given four options: Kennedy, Johnson, Nixon, and Reagan. Even if the plurality is able to identify the right answer (Nixon!), it is highly likely that Kennedy, Johnson, and Reagan will attract more total votes than Nixon will. And sometimes the plurality itself will blunder. I am willing to predict that pluralities of randomly selected groups of Americans would not select Nixon in the case just given. In short, statistical groups will err if confusion and ignorance are so widespread that individuals' answers are worse than random.

Here, too, there are evident applications to many contexts in business, politics, and law. Suppose that company employees are too optimistic about a new product, or that members of a legislature overstate the risks caused by certain pollutants, or that federal judges systematically err about scientific issues. If so, then the relevant judgments will be erroneous even if the beliefs of numerous people are being considered and averaged.

There is another problem. Interest groups will often be a source of error in the political domain. They will bring their power to bear, leading representatives in bad directions. Political blunders, and sometimes severe injustice, are the result. In the context of environmental protection, for example, powerful private groups have often been able to push Congress to favor their interests, such as coal production, even though pollution reduction is the nominal goal.[34]

Statistical Answers and Experts /

Should statistical averages be used more frequently than they now are? Do statistical averages outperform experts?

Everything depends on the competence of the experts. Suppose that we could find real experts on estimating the weight of oxen or on counting jelly beans; suppose, too, that we understand expertise to be the ability to make accurate assessments. If so, then these (admittedly weird and obsessive) experts would, by definition, do better than statistical averages. In the real world, we must often choose between a small group of people, each with a large amount of information, and a large group of people, each with a small amount of information. Sometimes the large group is worse.

Imagine that a group of people is trying to decide how many Supreme Court decisions have invalidated a state or federal law, or the number of lines in *Antigone*, or the weight of the most recent winner of the Kentucky Derby. Would it make the slightest sense to poll group members individually and to assume that the average response is accurate? If the group is large enough, the average answer will be quite good, at least if group members are not systematically biased and if many or most are more likely than not to be right. (I conducted such a poll with faculty at the University of Chicago Law School. We did exceedingly well in estimating the weight of the horse who last won the Kentucky Derby. We did fairly badly in estimating the number of lines in *Antigone*. We did horrendously with the number of Supreme Court invalidations of state and federal law.)

If experts are available, it would make sense to obtain a statistical answer from a group of them, rather than to select one or a few. If experts are likely to be right, a statistical group of experts should have exactly the same advantage over individual experts as a statistical group of ordinary people has over ordinary individuals. Many expert minds are likely to be better than a few. A great deal of evidence supports this claim.[35] Return to the 2004 baseball predictions described earlier; the judgments of statistical groups of baseball experts were uncannily accurate. Because those judgments were perfect as a group, they could not possibly be inferior to that of any individual expert.

There is more systematic evidence in this vein. In a series of thirty comparisons, statistical groups of experts had 12.5 percent fewer errors than individual experts on forecasting tasks involving such diverse issues as cattle and chicken prices, real and nominal GNP, survival of patients, and housing starts.[36] Statistical groups of experts significantly outperformed individual experts in predicting the annual earnings of firms, changes in the U.S. economy, and annual peak rainfall runoff.[37] For private and public institutions, the implication is straightforward: "Organizations often call on the best expert they can find to make important forecasts. They should avoid this practice, and instead combine forecasts from a number of experts."[38] (Leaders of companies and nations should take note.)

For political polling, it has become standard practice to combine a set of poll results and to rely on the average or median, rather than to select one or two. The most sophisticated treatment here involves Polly, a computer program designed to predict the results of the 2004 presidential election.[39] How did Polly do? In the exuberant words of Polly's manager:

> POLLY WAS RIGHT! Who would win in November—George W. Bush or John F. Kerry? This question consumed Polly since March, when her page was launched. She heard from many sources, including 268 polls, 10 forecasting models, three surveys over as many months of a select panel of American politics experts, and the Iowa Electronic Markets (IEM). . . . Averaging across methods . . . Polly calculated the *Pollyvote*, the share of the two-party vote (that is, omitting third-parties) that Bush was predicted to win. Once or twice a week our parrot would post the latest value of the Pollyvote on this page and, invariably, even as Bush's standing in the polls sank in July . . . this variable showed Bush would win on election day. Not once during the past eight months did the value of the Pollyvote dip below 50 percent. . . . Then, on the morning of November 2, Polly posted her final forecast: President Bush would take 51.5 percent of the two-party vote. This hit bull's eye! As far as Polly knows, no other forecast, by pollster, pundit, or scholar, got it exactly right.[40]

There is a general lesson here for predictions about electoral outcomes. In routine polling, forecasters often lack enough different polls on the same question; they might instead use multiple indicators, a range of diverse questions that tap into the same underlying sentiment. The answer might be averaged into some kind of composite, one that is likely to be more reliable than individual items.[41]

Might understandings of this kind be adapted for use in determining public policy? Compare in this regard the Copenhagen Consensus, generated by a group of economists in an attempt to inform policy judgments about global risks, that is, hazards faced by millions of people all over the world.[42] The Copenhagen Consensus emerged from an effort to evaluate a series of possible government interventions involving (among other problems) climate change, water and sanitation, hunger and malnutrition, free trade, and communicable diseases (including AIDS/HIV). Experts were asked about the best way to promote global welfare, particularly the welfare of developing countries, assuming that $50 billion was made available for that purpose. Each of the experts ranked the possible projects, allowing the production of an overall ranking (reflecting the average rankings of the experts taken as a whole). As it happens, climate change was lowest on the list, and addressing communicable diseases, reducing hunger and malnutrition, and free trade were at the top.

I do not mean to say that the results of this particular exercise are correct; everything depends on whether the relevant experts were in a position to offer good answers on the questions at hand. If the experts suffer from a systematic bias, or if their answers are worse than random, any effort to aggregate expert judgments will produce blunders. Maybe we shouldn't trust the people who participated in the Copenhagen Consensus. But if statistical averages are a good way to aggregate knowledge when ordinary people know something of relevance, then they are also a good way to aggregate knowledge from experts.[43]

/ No Magic Here /

At first glance, the accuracy of statistical judgments looks like a parlor trick or even a kind of magic. How can the average member of a large group of people turn out to "know" the number of beans in a jar, the weight of an animal, the likely winner of sports events, the outcome of future elections? We can now see that there's no magic here. The explanation lies in simple arithmetic and the Condorcet Jury Theorem. If most people are more likely than not to be right, then the average judgment of a a large collection of people will be uncannily accurate. And if those without knowledge make random errors, then large groups can also arrive at the truth simply because the average judgment will be determined by those who have relevant information.

But we can also specify the conditions under which groups, large or small, will certainly err. As Condorcet emphasized, those conditions are not difficult to find. In many domains, most people are not likely to be right, and their errors will be systematic rather than random.

Should policy be made by opinion polls? The Jury Theorem makes this question less senseless than it might at first seem. But for groups and institutions, including democratic ones, it would be wrong to suggest that the best approach to hard questions is to ask a large number of people and to take the average answer. That approach is likely to work only under distinctive circumstances: those in which many or most people are more likely than not to be right. Such circumstances might be found when, for example, a company president is asking a group of informed advisors about the proper course of action, or when a dean at a university is asking a faculty whether to hire a certain job candidate, or when a head of a government agency is consulting a group of scientists about whether a particular pollution problem is likely to be serious. In all of these cases, there is reason to trust the people who are being asked, and hence the average answer is peculiarly likely to be right.

But it would make no sense to make policy by asking everyone in the world whether the United States should sign the Kyoto Protocol, or whether genetic engineering poses serious risks, or whether a significant increase in the minimum wage would increase unemployment, or whether the death penalty has a deterrent effect on crime, or whether rent control policies help or hurt poor tenants. In these cases, there is a great risk that error and confusion at the individual level will be replicated at the level of group averages.

The implications for group behavior and democracy are mixed. To the extent that the goal is to arrive at the correct judgments on facts, the Condorcet Jury Theorem affords no guarantees. In numerous domains, too many people are likely to blunder in systematic ways. Indeed, well-functioning groups, and well-functioning democracies, fully recognize this point, and they delegate fact-finding authority to specialists who know what they are doing.

But for generalists as well as specialists, in the private sector and the public domain, an important question remains: Will deliberation help?

Chapter Two / **The Surprising Failures of Deliberating Groups**

Let us begin with three examples of deliberation in action.

1. In the summer of 2005, a small experiment in democracy was held in Colorado.[1] Sixty American citizens were brought together and assembled into ten groups, each consisting of five to seven people. Members of each group were asked to deliberate on three of the most controversial issues of the day: *Should states allow same-sex couples to enter into civil unions? Should employers engage in "affirmative action" by giving a preference to members of traditionally disadvantaged groups? Should the United States sign an international treaty to combat global warming?*

As the experiment was designed, the groups consisted of either "liberal" and "conservative" members, the former from Boulder, the latter from Colorado Springs. In the parlance of election years, there were five Blue State groups and five Red State groups: five groups whose members initially tended toward liberal positions on the three issues, and five whose members tended toward conservative positions on those issues. People were asked to state their opinions anonymously both before and after fifteen minutes of group discussion. What was the effect of discussion?

The results were simple. In almost every group, members ended up with more extreme positions after they spoke with one another. Discussion made civil unions more popular among liberals; discussion made civil unions less popular among conservatives. Liberals favored an international treaty to control global warming before discussion; they favored it more strongly after discussion. Conservatives were neutral on that treaty before discussion; they strongly opposed it after discussion. Mildly favorable toward affirmative action before discussion, liberals became strongly favorable toward affirmative action after discussion. Firmly negative about affirmative action before discussion, conservatives became even more negative about affirmative action after discussion.

Aside from increasing extremism, the experiment had an independent effect: It made both liberal groups and conservative groups significantly more homogeneous—and thus squelched diversity. Before members started to talk, many groups displayed a fair bit of internal disagreement. The disagreements were reduced as a result of a mere fifteen-minute discussion. Even in their anonymous statements, group members showed far more consensus after discussion than before.

It follows that discussion helped to widen the rift between liberals and conservatives on all three issues. Before discussion, some liberal groups were, on some issues, fairly close to some conservative groups. The result of discussion was to divide them far more sharply.

2. On April 17, 1961, the U.S. Navy, the U.S. Air Force, and the Central Intelligence Agency helped fifteen hundred Cuban exiles in an effort to invade Cuba at the Bay of Pigs. The invasion was a disaster.[2] The Cuban army, consisting of twenty thousand well-trained soldiers, killed a number of the invaders and captured most of the remaining twelve hundred. Two American supply ships were sunk by Cuban planes; two fled; four failed to arrive in time. The United

States was able to obtain release of the twelve hundred prisoners, but only in return for $53 million in foreign aid to Cuba, along with international opprobrium and a strengthening of relations between Cuba and the Soviet Union.

Soon after the failure, President Kennedy asked, "How could I have been so stupid to let them go ahead?"[3] The answer does not lie in the limitations of Kennedy's advisors, an exceptionally experienced and talented group. Indeed, the invasion of Cuba followed a lengthy process of deliberation, in which all participants were free to have their say. Some of Kennedy's advisors entertained private doubts, but they "never pressed, partly out of a fear of being labelled 'soft' or undaring in the eyes of their colleagues."[4] The failure to press those doubts mattered. According to Arthur Schlesinger Jr., a participant in the deliberations, Kennedy's "senior officials . . . were unanimous for going ahead. . . . Had one senior advisor opposed the adventure, I believe that Kennedy would have canceled it. No one spoke against it."[5]

3. A few years ago, more than three thousand people were brought together and assembled into more than five hundred mock juries, each consisting of six people.[6] Jurors were given a videotaped narration of a personal injury case, along with a written case summary and instructions. Initially, each juror was asked to record a written opinion entirely in private, offering a view about the appropriate punitive award against the wrongdoer. Thereafter, jurors were asked to talk together and to reach a verdict. What was the effect of deliberation?

The answer is that it produced substantial shifts. Almost every jury ended up choosing a higher award than that favored by the median juror in advance of deliberation. In fully 27 percent of the cases, the jury selected an award that was as high as, or even higher than, that of the highest individual juror before deliberation began! In short, deliberation produced a significant shift toward more severe punishment.

Whatever we make of these particular examples, it is easy to imagine that a deliberating group would do a lot better than a statistical aggregation of private judgments. In theory, a deliberating group should perform well even if some of its members are error-prone. Deliberation, in the form of an exchange of information and reasons, might well bring them into line. In a deliberating group, everyone should end up knowing what each individual knows, and the whole should be at least the sum of the parts. If we want to elicit all available information, deliberation might seem the most promising route.

Suppose that many group members give answers that are worse than random. If so, other group members can show them how they have erred. If some officials have exaggerated a threat from another country, underestimated the risk of a hurricane, or misunderstood the will of the public, perhaps deliberation will correct their mistakes. If people have been manipulated in their private judgments, perhaps deliberation will undo the effects of the manipulation. A nation's leaders often try to convince citizens that the economy is improving, but deliberation might reveal that the economy is actually getting worse. If some group members have anchored on a misleading value, perhaps deliberation will expose the anchor as such. A plaintiff's lawyer might ask a jury to give a $1 million award for a libel of a famous movie star, but deliberation might show that the star, upset though he may be, has not really been injured to the tune of $1 million.

/ Theory and Practice /

This optimistic view can be traced to Aristotle, who suggested that when diverse groups "all come together . . . they may surpass—collectively and as a body, although not individually—the quality of the few best. . . . When there are many who contribute to the process of deliberation, each can bring his share of goodness and moral prudence . . . some appreciate one part, some another, and all together appreciate all."[7] Here, then, is a clear suggestion that many minds, deliberating together, may improve on "the quality of the few best."

More recently, John Rawls wrote of the same possibility: "The benefits from discussion lie in the fact that even representative legislators are limited in knowledge and the ability to reason. No one of them knows everything the others know, or can make all the same inferences that they can draw in concert. Discussion is a way of combining information and enlarging the range of arguments."[8] Rawls is alert to the dispersed nature of knowledge and the possibility that deliberation among diverse people can have significant benefits. I have mentioned Habermas's emphasis on processes of deliberation in which the "forceless force of the better argument" should prevail.

Understandings of this kind are not merely theoretical; they even help to illuminate the design of the U.S. Constitution. We have seen that the Constitution attempts to create a deliberative democracy, in the form of a system that combines accountability to the people with reflection and reason giving. James Madison himself described the Constitutional Convention as a highly deliberative arena, in which "no man felt himself obliged to retain his opinions any longer than he was satisfied of their propriety and truth, and was open to the force of argument."[9] In a deliberative democracy, the exercise of public power must be justified by legitimate reasons, not merely by the will of some segment of society, and indeed not merely by the will of the majority, whatever the Jury Theorem may say. For the United States at least, a key goal of a deliberative democracy is to ensure that widely dispersed information is obtained and incorporated into public decisions.

The very structure of the U.S. government, with its bicameral legislature and its complex allocation of authority among the three branches, can be seen as an effort to ensure a high degree of deliberation with reference to relevant information, as well as a large measure of accountability. The system of free expression and the metaphor of the "marketplace of ideas" should be understood in deliberative terms. Indeed, both the opponents and the advocates of the U.S. Constitution were firmly committed to political deliberation. They considered themselves republicans, seeking a high degree of self-government without embracing pure populism.

The possibility of having a republican form of government in a nation with many minds, in the form of a large and heterogeneous citizenry, generated intense controversy in the founding period. The American framers' largest innovation consisted not in their emphasis on deliberation, which was uncontested at the time, but in their fear of homogeneity, their enthusiasm for disagreement and diversity, and their effort to accommodate and to structure that diversity. The antifederalists, opponents of the proposed Constitution, thought that the framers' project was doomed. The antifederalist Brutus insisted that the people "should be similar" and feared that without similarity, "there will be constant clashing of opinions."[10] In response, the framers welcomed such clashing and urged that the "jarring of parties" would "promote deliberation and circumspection." In their view, a constitution that ensures the "jarring of parties" and "differences of opinion" would "promote deliberation."[11]

A similar point emerges from one of the most illuminating early debates, raising the question whether the Bill of Rights should include a "right to instruct" representatives. That right was defended with the claim that citizens of a particular region ought to have the authority to bind their representatives about how to vote. And if we emphasize the likely correctness of the average view of a large group of people, the right to instruct would seem to make a great deal of sense. Indeed, that right might appear to ensure that the outcome of debates would be determined by the average view—an embodiment of the high hopes of the Condorcet Jury Theorem. (Recall, however, that Condorcet himself gave reason for skepticism about this view, urging that decisions should be delegated to enlightened representatives.) In rejecting the right to instruct in the founding era, Roger Sherman made the decisive argument: "The words are calculated to mislead the people, by conveying an idea that they have a right to control the debates of the Legislature. This cannot be admitted to be just, because it would destroy the object of their meeting. I think, when the people have chosen a representative, it is his duty to meet others from the different parts of the Union, and consult, and agree with them on such acts as are for the general benefit of the whole community. If they were to be guided by instructions, there would be no use in deliberation."[12]

Sherman's words reflect the founders' enthusiasm for deliberation among representatives who are numerous and diverse and who disagree on issues both large and small. Indeed, it was through deliberation among such persons that "such acts as are for the general benefit of the whole community" would emerge.

The American founding to one side, history and practice attest to the widespread belief that deliberation is likely to improve judgments, and that it should be greatly preferred to simple aggregations of opinion and belief. In countless domains, deliberation is our favored method for arriving at the correct answer. Certainly this has long been true in legislatures and workplaces and on corporate boards; it is also true for judicial panels and in academic life. No one doubts that deliberative processes have often done a lot of good. The question is whether some such processes do better than others, and whether it is really sensible to celebrate deliberation in the abstract. I will be raising a number of doubts about such celebrations.

To make the analysis tractable, let us focus on how deliberating groups might be able to answer factual questions or to solve puzzles that really have solutions. If such groups do badly in such contexts, there is no reason to think that they will do well in answering questions for which there is no consensus on truth or validity.

For obvious reasons, I focus on studies of deliberation within small groups rather than large ones. It is not so easy to study a genuinely deliberative process among a thousand people (though, as we shall see, new technologies make this more feasible every day). The outcomes of deliberations within small groups tell us a lot about what will happen as the size of the group expands.

Why Deliberation Might Work /
If statistical groups do well, we might be tempted to think that deliberating groups will do extremely well. And if Aristotle and Rawls are right, the very fact of deliberation is

a virtue rather than a vice. If groups perform better than their average member, we can imagine three principal mechanisms by which the improvement might occur.

Groups as Equivalent to Their Best Members / Groups might equal the performance of their best members. One or more group members often know the right answer, and other group members might well become convinced of this fact. If some or many members suffer from ignorance, or from a form of bias that leads to error, other group members might correct them. This is the simple idea that "truth wins."

Almost everyone has had the experience of participating in a group discussion in which one or another person knows the truth. Which countries fought alongside Hitler in World War II? How are leaders chosen in Japan? Who won the Academy Award for best actress last year? Who was president of the United States in 1952? If one person knows, everyone else is likely to end up knowing, too. Consider a mundane example from the faculty of the University of Chicago Law School. A number of faculty members were asked their individual judgments about the number of students at the University of Chicago Laboratory Schools, which runs from kindergarten through high school. The average judgment was fairly close, within a few hundred of the right answer, which was seventeen hundred. After a brief deliberative process, the group converged on the right answer for this reason: One faculty member knew it, and he was able to convince everyone else that he did.

Suppose that a group of military officials is attempting to assess the strengths and weaknesses of a terrorist group operating in Southeast Asia. If one of them is a specialist in military affairs in that region, all of them can learn what the specialist knows. Many deliberating groups contain at least one expert on the question at hand; if group members listen to the expert, they will do at least as well as the expert does. Of course, deliberation should not be confused with deference to experts. But genuine deliberation and reason giving might correct individual errors, rather than propagating them, in a way that allows convergence on the judgment of the most accurate group member.

Aggregation / Deliberation could aggregate information and ideas in a way that leads the group as a whole to know even more, and to do even better, than its best member does. Suppose that the group contains no experts on the question at issue, but that a fair bit of information is dispersed among group members. If those members consult with one another, the group may turn out to be expert even if its members are not. No individual person may know how to fix a malfunctioning car, to build a better mousetrap, or to repair a broken computer, but the group as a whole may well have the necessary information. Or suppose that the group contains a number of specialists, but that each member is puzzled about how to solve a particular problem, involving, say, the most effective way to respond to a natural disaster or the right approach to marketing a new product. Deliberation might elicit perspectives and information and thus allow the group to make an excellent judgment.

In this process, the whole is equal to the sum of the parts—and the sum of the parts is exactly what is sought. This is one reading of Aristotle's suggestion that a group may do significantly better than the few best.

Synergy and Learning / The give-and-take of group discussion might sift information and perspectives in a way that leads the group to a good solution to a problem, one in which the whole is actually *more* than the sum of its parts. In such cases, deliberation is, at the very least, an ambitious form of information aggregation, in which the exchange of views leads to a creative answer or solution that no member could generate individually.

There is another possibility. Some of the time, deliberation will create a process of synergy or learning, spurring creativity and producing an outcome that is far better than a mere aggregation of preexisting knowledge. In fact, groups sometimes do outperform their best members, in a way that suggests that synergy is involved.[13]

Confident and Unified /

To what extent do these mechanisms work in practice? Before answering that question, consider two points that are entirely clear. First, group members tend to become a lot more confident about their judgments after speaking with one another.[14] A key effect of group interaction is a greater sense that the postdeliberation conclusion is correct—whether or not it actually is.[15] Why does deliberation have this effect? A major reason is that we are more confident about our judgments after they have been corroborated by others,[16] an important point to which I will return.

Second, deliberation usually promotes uniformity by decreasing the range of views within groups.[17] After talking together, group members come into greater accord with one another.[18] Recall the Colorado experiment discussed earlier; both liberal and conservative group members showed greater homogeneity on global warming, affirmative action, and civil unions for same-sex couples. A central effect of deliberation is to reduce (squelch?) the range of opinions. It is for this reason that statistical groups show far more diversity of opinion than deliberating groups.

How should we evaluate these increases in confidence and unity? If the purpose of deliberation is not simply to produce accurate outcomes, then it might be wonderful to see that deliberation ensures more uniformity and higher confidence. Suppose that a key goal of deliberation is to promote a sense of *legitimacy*: an appreciation, by many people, that they have been able to participate in the process accompanied by a belief, on the part of all concerned, that the decision is right. Because deliberation increases uniformity and confidence in the outcome, it might be favored even if it produces errors. Imagine that a company is embarking on some fresh project, or that a local government is venturing a new initiative to protect the environment. If everyone is both confident and on board, success may well become more likely. Indeed, the group's enthusiasm might increase the chance of a good outcome even if another course of action would have been better.

But suppose that deliberation is leading to a worse decision. We might still be willing to accept a little more error if that is the price for more uniformity and greater confidence. If deliberation significantly increases the sense of legitimacy, then it might be desirable even if the decision is slightly inferior, at least if little turns on slight differences in the quality of the outcome. Perhaps what most matters is that many minds accept the decision, not that the decision be correct.

On the other hand, an increase in legitimacy might not be so important if the decision is leading the group to make a big blunder. If deliberation makes a nation less prepared to handle a natural disaster, deliberation may not be so great even if the deliberators are both confident and unified. For many decisions, the key goal of deliberation is to improve choices, not to legitimate whatever choice ultimately is made. And if deliberation can improve outcomes while also increasing legitimacy, so much the better.

Do Deliberators Make Accurate Decisions? /

Now let us turn to the most important question, which is whether deliberation leads people to good decisions. To answer that question, we need to establish some kind of baseline, allowing us to compare the postdeliberation outcome with something else. The most ambitious baseline is the truth: Do deliberators reach the correct result? A less ambitious baseline is the appropriate aggregation of the information that group members actually have: Do deliberators take good account of the information that is dispersed within the group? A still less ambitious baseline is provided by statistical groups: Do deliberating groups do better, or worse, than such groups?

The Basic Story / Unfortunately, there is no systematic evidence that deliberating groups do well by *any* of these three baselines.[19] I shall be offering a complex story, but here are the major lessons:

1. It cannot be shown that deliberating groups generally arrive at the truth. As we shall see, the truth is likely to win only when the correct view has a lot of support within the group before people start to talk. If the correct view does not have such advance support, the group will arrive at the truth only on questions for which the correct answer, once announced, is clearly right, and appears clearly right to everyone.
2. Much of the time, deliberating groups do quite poorly at aggregating the information that their members

have. When many minds get together, they often fail to learn nearly as much as they might. Relevant knowledge is often ignored or downplayed, above all because information known in advance by all or most group members has a far greater role than information that is known by only one or a few group members.

3. Deliberating groups sometimes outperform statistical groups, but sometimes the opposite is the case. When individuals show a strong bias or a clear tendency toward error, deliberating groups often show a greater bias and hence a greater tendency toward error. And because members of deliberating groups emphasize shared knowledge at the expense of unshared knowledge, they sometimes fail to take advantage of information that emerges from surveys and polls. A simple but somewhat chilling finding: In tasks where the right answer cannot easily be shown to be correct, groups tend to be *more* biased than individuals— except when the individual bias is very weak, or so strong that it cannot be further amplified![20]

Taken as a whole, these findings present an extremely serious problem for the optimistic view of Aristotle and Rawls, and indeed for all others who favor deliberation as a method for improving judgments. Such problems even suggest that deliberation on the Internet (as, for example, through blogs) can produce errors and nonsense. When like-minded people cluster, they often aggravate their biases, spreading falsehoods. At a minimum, these points suggest that it is important to take self-conscious steps to increase the likelihood that deliberation will profit from what the deliberators know.

Deliberating Groups and Statistical Groups / Let us begin with a clean test of the least ambitious claim, which is that deliberating groups will outperform statistical groups.[21] If deliberating groups do well by this baseline, we have reason to use them, rather than surveys, in real-world situations. But if deliberating groups do badly by this baseline, we have reason to be nervous about them and to investigate the source of the problem.

People were asked a range of (pretty dull) questions about the relationship between height or weight on the one hand and likely sex on the other. For example: "The observed height of a person is sixty-eight inches. Is the person more likely to be a male or a female? How much more likely?" Or: "The observed weight of a person is 130 pounds. Is the person more likely to be a male or a female?" Different groups of similar people were asked to answer such questions through different methods. In one method, people were asked to deliberate together about the likely answers and then to make individual estimates. In another, people were simply asked to make individual estimates in an effort to test the optimistic view suggested by the Condorcet Jury Theorem. A comparison of the two provides a simple test of whether deliberation improves judgment. The main result is that deliberation produced *no* systematic improvement. For half of the eight questions, deliberation produced worse, not better, outcomes than emerged from individual estimates. Overall, statistical groups and interacting groups did about the same.

This finding is typical. With respect to questions with definite answers, deliberating groups tend to do about as well as or slightly better than their average member, but not as well as their best members.[22] One study does find that when asked to estimate the populations of U.S. cities, groups did as well as their most accurate individual member;[23] but in the vast majority of studies, this does not happen.[24] Hence it is false to say that group members usually end up deferring to their internal specialists. Deliberating groups and statistical groups often do about equally well (or poorly).

For example, no significant differences are found between deliberating groups and average individual performances in numerical estimates involving the number of beans in a jar or the length of lines.[25] Another study tested whether deliberating groups were particularly good at telling whether people were telling the truth or lying.[26] The individual votes, predeliberation, were 48 percent correct, about the same as the postdeliberation judgments. Approximately the same number of people shifted toward error as toward correct answers. Yet another study finds that in various brainteasers, groups did better than their average member, but not as well as their best member.[27] Several studies find that in estimating quantities, groups do about as well as their average member, and worse than their best member.[28]

What about brainstorming problems, in which group members are charged with developing new ideas? Here deliberation can be positively harmful. For such problems, deliberating groups have been found to do far less well than statistical groups. The apparent reason is that deliberating groups discourage novelty.[29] Hence, "brainstorming is actually most beneficial when carried out initially in *private,* the interacting group then being used as a forum for combining and evaluating these individually produced ideas."[30]

When Deliberation Works: Eureka Problems / For advocates of deliberation, there is some good news. On crossword puzzles and similar problems, groups do tend to perform better than most individuals. Happily, they engage in a process of information aggregation and mutual error correction.[31] The most important finding here is that deliberating groups do well on "eureka" questions: those with answers that are self-affirming or that are clearly right once stated. There is a large lesson here for circumstances in which private and public organizations might do well to use deliberation.

For eureka problems, a single correct member usually ensures a correct answer from the group.[32] And if the question has a readily demonstrable answer, it is more likely that groups will converge on it.[33] Suppose that the question is how many people were on the earth in 1940, or the year in which a human being first walked on the moon, or the distance between Paris and London. Suppose, too, that one or a few people in a deliberating group know the right answer. If so, there is a good chance that the group will accept that answer.[34]

When this is so, the reason is simple: The person who knows the answer will speak with assurance and authority, and she is likely to be convincing for that very reason. An early study finds that those with correct answers are usually more confident, and confidence is "associated with correctness for both individual and group performance."[35] Consider in this light the finding that pairs tend to do better than individuals on tests involving general vocabulary knowledge; those pairs with at least one high-ability member, who tended to be confident, generally performed at the same level as their more competent member.[36]

Evidence in the same vein comes from a striking finding by economists David Cooper and John Kagel that deliberating groups do better than individuals in a complex game of economic strategy.[37] In that game, people are asked to be monopolists, with the goal of deterring new entry by signaling that they will be tough competitors. The game has a feature in common with the eureka problems on which deliberating teams do well; once the solution is discovered, participants have a shared reaction of "Aha!" Cooper and Kagel used a baseline under which group performance would be measured by seeing if groups did as well as their best member. Their basic finding is that teams usually did as well as their best member or even better. With especially difficult strategic problems, the difference between groups and individuals was even more pronounced in favor of the former.

Another study finds that groups performed exceedingly well, far better than individual members, in two complex tasks that had demonstrably correct solutions.[38] The first involved a statistical problem, requiring subjects to guess the composition of an urn containing blue balls and red balls. The second involved a problem in monetary policy, asking participants to manipulate the interest rate to steer the economy in good directions. People were asked to perform as individuals and in groups. The basic results for the two experiments were similar: Groups significantly outper-formed individuals. Interestingly, groups did not, on balance, take longer to make a decision. In terms of both accuracy and time, there were no differences between group decisions made with a unanimity requirement and group decisions made by majority rule.

How can these good results be explained? An obvious possibility is that the group's discussion is simply the average of individual judgments. On this view, the judgments of these deliberating groups simply *were* statistical judgments. But the evidence is inconsistent with this hypothesis; groups in these cases did far better than their average member. An alternative hypothesis is that each group contained one or more strong analysts who were able to move the group in the right direction. But in the experiments, there is little support for this hypothesis either.[39]

It seems that, in these experiments, the better decisions by groups resulted from the fact that the best points and arguments spread among the various individual players. Here we find some basis for the Aristotelian claim that, under appropriate conditions, groups can do much better than individuals. The relevant conditions appear to include highly competent group members attempting to solve statistical problems that all members know to have demonstrably correct answers.

In the same vein, some evidence suggests that although deliberating groups often fail to spread information, they are less likely to neglect unshared information *if they believe that there is a demonstrably correct answer to the question they are trying to answer.*[40] Asked to solve a murder mystery, a deliberating group did far better when its members were told that they had sufficient clues to "determine" the identity of the guilty suspect than when they were told to decide which suspect was "most likely to have committed the crime."[41] Those who believe that they are solving a problem with a correct solution are more likely to explore dispersed information than those who think that they are simply reaching a consensus. Even here, however, at least a few others in the group must show some initial support for the member who knows the right solution; if not, the group frequently will fail.[42]

The most general point in favor of deliberation is that a deliberating group will converge on the truth, and outperform statistical groups as well, *if* the truth has some initial social support within the group *and* when the task has a demonstrably correct answer according to a framework that group members share.[43] When groups outperform most of their individual members, the issue must usually be one on which a particular answer can be shown, to the satisfaction of all or most, to be right. A math problem, or a problem of simple logic, is an example. If one group member really knows calculus, others are likely to accept that member's judgment. But even for such problems, the group might not do well if the demonstrably correct solution lacks significant support at the outset.[44]

Predictions and Celebrations / Is it possible to predict how a group's judgment after deliberation will compare to the initial judgments of its individual members? For many tasks, simple majority schemes do fairly well at predicting group judgments. The group often does what the majority wants. It follows that if the majority is wrong, the group will probably be wrong as well.[45]

Most generally, a comprehensive study demonstrated that majority pressures can be powerful even for factual questions on which some people know the right answer.[46] The study involved twelve hundred people, forming groups of six, five, and four members. Individuals were asked true/false questions involving art, poetry, public opinion, geography, economics, and politics. They were then asked to assemble into groups, which discussed the questions and produced answers by consensus. The clearest result was that the views of the majority played a big role in determining the group's answers. When a majority of individuals in the group gave the right answer, the group's decision followed the majority in no less than 79 percent of the cases!

The truth played a role, too, but a lesser one. If a majority of individuals in the group gave the wrong answer, the group decision nonetheless moved toward the majority position in 56 percent of the cases. Hence, the truth did have an influence—79 percent is higher than 56 percent—and this is a definite point in favor of deliberation. But the majority's judgment, and not the truth, was the dominant influence. And because the majority was influential even when wrong, the average group decision was right only slightly more often than the average individual decision (66 percent vs. 62 percent).

What is most important is that groups did not perform as well as they would have if they had properly aggregated the information that group members possessed. The underutilization of information is even more pronounced in highly cohesive groups with a shared sense of identity.[47] In such groups, information is peculiarly unlikely to be revealed. It follows that in many deliberating groups—consisting, say, of people with a defined political view—mutual interaction will not do much to elicit the information that members actually have.

The same general conclusion holds with experts. As a result, statistical aggregations, based on independent views, are usually better than standard group meetings, where information is not used efficiently.[48] Let us now turn to the most general sources of deliberative failure, understood as a failure to make accurate decisions on the basis of the information that group members actually have.

Two Sources of Deliberative Failure: Informational Influences and Social Pressures /

When statistical groups do well, it is because people say what they think. But with deliberating groups, this might not happen. Exposure to the views of others might lead people to silence themselves, and for two different reasons.

Information / The first reason involves the informational signals provided by the acts and views of other people. Suppose that most people in your group believe that some proposition is true; they might believe that a hurricane is unlikely to hit a city, that there is no connection between cell phone use and automobile accidents, that a terrorist attack is likely in the next year, that a certain politician has committed a crime. If most people think one of these things, you have reason to agree with them. How can most people be wrong? Your trust in the judgment of others might outweigh any private reason that you have for believing that the proposition is false, and hence you might simply defer.

If most group members share a particular belief, other members, or those with a minority view, might not speak out simply because they are willing to respect the informational signal given by the statements of others. Many political judgments are influenced in this way. If you find yourself in a deliberating group whose members believe that global warming is a serious problem, or that a war effort in some nation is going well, or that a political leader is corrupt, you might well learn from what they say and move in their direction.

Not surprisingly, the strength of the informational signal will depend on the number and nature of the people who are giving it. Most people really don't like being the sole dissenter. If all but one person in a deliberating group have said that some proposition is true, then the remaining member may well agree that the proposition is true—even to the point of ignoring the evidence of his or her own senses. Solomon Asch established the point in his famous and somewhat alarming experiments involving the length of lines, in which most people were willing, at least once, to defy the evidence of their own eyes and to defer to the group's clearly false judgments.[49] And if the group contains one or more people who are well-known to be authorities, then other group members are all the more likely to defer to them.[50] People are much more willing to say what they know if other dissenters are present and if a principle of equality is widely accepted within the group.

Here, then, is an important clue about why deliberating groups fail to arrive at truth, do not aggregate the information that group members actually have, and often cannot even outperform statistical groups. If members are listening to one another, they might defer to leaders or to the apparent consensus and thus silence themselves. The implications for actual group behavior are clear. We have seen that in the United States, government agencies failed to use relevant information about weapons of mass destruction in Iraq and the risks posed by the flight of the Columbia space shuttle. Informational signals played a large role. Whenever an organization falls prey to groupthink, such signals are likely to be at work. The same point helps to explain "political correctness." If students and faculty on university campuses move to the left, it may well be because most people have left-wing views, and other students and faculty shift accordingly. Widely held left-wing opinions carry weight, especially if they are supported by respected authorities; it should be no surprise if people move in the direction of their views. Of course conservative opinions can spread in exactly the same way.

Social Influences / The second problem for deliberation involves social influences. If people fear that their statements will be disliked or ridiculed, they might not speak out, even on questions of fact. Their silence might stem not from a belief that they are wrong, as in the case of informational pressure, but instead from the fear of social punishment. Many people silence themselves because they do not want to look stupid or to create trouble. When deliberating groups do not arrive at the truth, or when they fail to aggregate information, self-silencing is often the key problem. And when deliberating groups do less well than statistical groups, it is usually because in the latter, unlike the former, people really say what they think.

In the most extreme cases, those who defy the collective wisdom face criminal punishment, at least in societies that do not respect free speech; a different kind of danger is exclusion from the group. At the very least, those who defy the dominant position will risk a form of disapproval that will lead them to be less trusted, liked, and respected in the future. When you find that someone agrees with you, you're apt to like that person more. In fact, when you find that someone agrees with you, you're apt to like *yourself* more as well. These facts can impose a lot of pressure on those who disclose information that is inconsistent with the group's consensus.

Of course, a large majority will impose more social pressure than a small one. And if certain group members are leaders or authorities, willing and able to impose punishments of various sorts, others will be unlikely to defy them publicly. In a deliberating group in which the leader is known to favor a particular decision and to dislike opposing views, relevant information is unlikely to be obtained. So too if the group is especially cohesive; in groups of that kind, social pressures are particularly intense.

Consider the striking fact that investment clubs have little dissent, and lose a lot of money, when members are united by close social ties.[51] Hence the robust finding that cohesive groups tend to decide poorly, among other things because they censor those who offer competing views.[52] When deliberating groups do badly, fear of social sanctions is often a major reason.

A Framework: Private Benefits versus Social Benefits / These points about deliberation can be put into a more general framework. Suppose that group members are deliberating about some factual question; suppose, too, that each member has some information that bears on the answer to that question. Will members disclose what they know?

For each person, the answer may well depend on the individual benefits and the individual costs of disclosure. Suppose that you disclose what you know about a problem that your company is facing. If you do, it is possible that you will receive only a fraction of the benefits that come from an improved decision by the group. And if each group member thinks this way, the group will receive only a fraction of the available information. When this is true, participants in deliberation face a standard collective action problem in which each person, following his or her rational self-interest, will tell the group less than it needs to know.

At least this is so under the assumption that each member will receive only a small portion of the benefits that come to the group from a good outcome—a plausible view about the situation facing many institutions, including corporate boards, workplaces, administrative agencies, and even the White House. There is a lesson here about how to improve deliberation. Suppose that group members are rewarded for telling the truth or for moving the group in a direction that turns out to be the right one. If so, then deliberation is likely to benefit from the knowledge of many more minds—an issue to which I turn in chapter 6.

Now suppose that the statements of others lead you to think that your own views are wrong or unhelpful. If so, then the private benefit of disclosure is reduced even more. In that event, you have reason to believe that disclosure won't improve the group's decision at all. Things are even worse if those who speak against the apparent consensus will suffer reputational injury (or more). In that event, the private calculus is straightforward: Silence really is golden.

So Many Minds, So Many Blunders /

Both informational pressure and social influences help to explain the striking finding that in a deliberating group, those with a minority position often silence themselves or otherwise have disproportionately little weight.[53] There is a more particular finding: Members of groups suffering from low social status—less educated people, sometimes women—speak less and carry less influence within deliberating groups than their higher-status peers.[54]

Why is this? The simplest answer is that both informational influence and social pressures are likely to be especially strong for low-status members. The unfortunate consequence is a loss of information to the group as a whole, ensuring that deliberating groups do far less well than they would if only they could aggregate the information held by group members.

Informational influences and social pressures help explain some otherwise puzzling findings about judicial voting on federal courts of appeals. It turns out that like-minded judges end up with more extreme opinions after they speak with one another. On three-judge panels, Republican appointees show especially conservative voting patterns when sitting with two other Republican appointees, and Democratic appointees show especially liberal voting patterns when sitting with two other Democratic appointees.[55] Consider, too, the finding that, when sitting with two Republican appointees, Democratic appointees show fairly conservative voting patterns, quite close to those of Republican appointees in the aggregate data. And when sitting with two Democratic appointees, Republican appointees are fairly liberal, with overall votes like those of Democratic appointees. For federal judges, informational pressure and social influences are not the whole story, but they play a big role.

Most ambitiously, we might think that the same forces help to explain the rise of culture itself, and hence to illuminate cultural differences among groups and nations that might not be expected to be fundamentally different from one another.[56] If individuals affect one another, and if judgments and errors can spread from a few to many, then seemingly small differences are likely to be magnified through social influences. Even with respect to political issues, involving human rights and related questions, deliberation can produce significant cross-cultural differences as a result of modest variations in neighbors and starting points.[57] And if such differences emerge, there is no reason for confidence that good judgments are emerging from deliberation as such—even if many minds are involved.

/ A Broader Question /

It is now time to ask a much broader question: Do these points amount to a challenge to deliberation as an ideal and as a practice? If so, what kind of challenge?

Many of those interested in deliberation have attempted to specify its preconditions in a way that is intended to ensure against some of the problems that I have been emphasizing here. Habermas, for example, stresses norms and practices designed to allow victory by "the better argument": "Rational discourse is supposed to be public and inclusive, to grant equal communication rights for participants, to require sincerity and to diffuse any kind of force other than the forceless force of the better argument. This communicative structure is expected to create a deliberative space for the mobilization of the best available contributions for the most relevant topics."[58]

In Habermas's famous "ideal speech situation," all participants attempt to seek the truth; they do not behave strategically; they accept a norm of equality.[59] Other advocates of deliberative democracy have spoken similarly about what appropriate deliberation entails.[60] On this view, deliberation, properly understood, does not simply involve the exchange of words and opinions. It imposes its own requirements and preconditions. Indeed, deliberation has its own internal morality, one that should overcome some of the harmful effects of deliberative processes in the real world. Perhaps deliberation will work well, and produce accurate results, when it follows that internal morality.

It is right to say that deliberation, properly understood, contains an internal morality that can be invoked to challenge processes that only purport to be deliberative. Suppose that the U.S. Senate is deliberating about some issue, such as the risk of terrorism, the problem of global warming, protection in the event of natural disasters, the confirmation of federal judges, or the appropriate response to water pollution in the Great Lakes. Suppose that the leaders of the majority party are firmly committed in advance to a certain outcome, so that they will not listen to the minority at all and even dissenting members of their own party will not be much heard. This is a parody of deliberation even if everyone is allowed to talk. Under these circumstances, it is impossible to get the benefit of many minds. Or suppose that members of a deliberating group do not much listen to African Americans or to women. If so, real deliberation cannot occur.

It is exceedingly important to satisfy preconditions of the sort identified by defenders of deliberation. Unfortunately, compliance with such preconditions will not cure the problems on which I focus here. Those problems are likely to arise among many minds even if discourse is public and inclusive, even if participants are sincere, and even if everyone has equal rights. The problems have distinctive structures; let us now turn to them.

Chapter Three / **Four Big Problems**

In Colorado, deliberation made liberals more liberal on global warming, affirmative action, and civil unions for same-sex couples; it also made conservatives more conservative. At least one of these sets of shifts must have been wrong. For both liberals and conservatives, deliberation could not possibly have reflected full use of dispersed information.

As we shall now see, deliberating groups typically suffer from four problems. They amplify the errors of their members. They do not elicit the information that their members have. They are subject to cascade effects, producing a situation in which the blind lead the blind. Finally, they show a tendency to group polarization, by which groups go to extremes. Each of these problems threatens to dash the hopes of those who want deliberating groups to take advantage of dispersed information. As a result, deliberation often fails to ensure that groups end up knowing what their members know; recall the cases of the CIA and NASA.

/ Amplifying Errors /

It is well-known that human beings do not always process information well. We use heuristics, or rules of thumb, that lead us to make predictable errors. We are also subject to identifiable biases, which can produce big mistakes.[1]

A growing literature explores the role of these heuristics and biases and their relationship to law and policy. For example, people err because they use the *availability heuristic* to answer difficult questions about probability. How likely is a terrorist attack, a hurricane, a traffic jam, an accident from a nuclear power plant, a case of venereal disease? When people use the availability heuristic, they answer a question of probability by asking whether examples come readily to mind.[2] The point very much bears on private and public responses to risks—suggesting, for example, that people will be especially responsive to the dangers of AIDS, crime, earthquakes, and nuclear power plant accidents if examples are easy to recall. The point also explains some of the sources of discrimination on the basis of race, sex, age, and disability. If it is easy for an employer to bring to mind cases in which a female employee quit work to care for her family, the employer is more likely to engage in sex discrimination in the future; the same is true for racial discrimination if it is easy to think of cases in which African American employees performed poorly.

In this way, *familiarity* can affect the availability of instances. But *salience* is important as well. A terrorist attack on television will be highly salient to viewers and will have a greater impact than a report about the attack in the newspaper.[3] Similarly, earlier events will have a smaller impact than more recent ones. The point helps explain much behavior. For example, whether people will buy insurance for natural disasters is greatly affected by recent experiences.[4] In the aftermath of an earthquake, people become far readier to buy insurance for earthquakes, but their readiness to do so declines steadily from that point, as vivid memories recede. Use of the availability heuristic is not irrational, but it can easily lead to serious errors of fact. After the 2005 disaster produced by Hurricane Katrina in the United States, it was predictable that significant steps would be taken to prepare for hurricanes—and also predictable that before that disaster, such steps would be quite inadequate.

Most people are also strikingly vulnerable to *framing effects*, making different decisions depending on the wording of the problem. Consider the question whether to undergo a risky medical procedure. When people are told, "Of those who have this procedure, 90 percent are alive after five years," they are far more likely to agree to the procedure than when they are told, "Of those who have this procedure, 10 percent are dead after five years."[5]

People also follow the *representativeness heuristic*, in accordance with which our judgments of probability are influenced by assessments of resemblance: the extent to which A "looks like" B.[6] If A does indeed look like B, we are more likely to think that A causes B, or vice versa. The representativeness heuristic can lead us to make *conjunction errors*, by which we believe that A-and-B are more likely to be true than either A or B alone. The most famous example involves the likely career of a hypothetical woman named Linda, described as follows: "Linda is thirty-one years old, single, outspoken, and very bright. She majored in philosophy. As a student, she was deeply concerned with issues of discrimination and social justice and also participated in antinuclear demonstrations." People were asked to rank, in order of probability, eight possible futures for Linda. Six of these were fillers (psychiatric social worker, elementary school teacher); the two crucial ones were "bank teller" and "bank teller and active in the feminist movement." In many experiments, many people said that Linda is less likely to be a bank teller than to be both a bank teller and active in the feminist movement. This is a palpable (though common!) error of logic;[7] it simply cannot be the case that A (bank teller) is less likely than A and B together (bank teller and active in the feminist movement). The representativeness heuristic often works well because it frequently points in the right direction; but it can also lead to severe blunders.

For purposes of assessing deliberation, a central question is whether deliberating groups avoid the errors of the individuals who compose them. We have seen that when most people err, statistical groups will err, too; this is an example of the dark side of the Condorcet Jury Theorem. Unfortunately, there is no clear evidence that deliberating groups eliminate the effects of heuristics and biases. On the contrary, there is considerable evidence that they do not. This is a vivid illustration of the principle "Garbage in, garbage out" in a way that mocks the aspiration to correction of individual blunders through deliberation. In fact, individual errors are not merely replicated but are actually amplified in group decisions, a process of "some garbage in, much garbage out." The most general finding is that deliberation can help when biases are held by one or a few group members, but that when a bias is widely shared, group interactions will actually increase its effect.[8]

Suppose, for example, that individual jurors are biased for some reason. Perhaps there has been pretrial publicity, misleadingly implicating the defendant (a famous movie star?) by placing him at the scene of the crime; perhaps the jury's bias is a product of the unappealing physical appearance of the defendant (not a famous movie star). If so, the many minds on the jury are likely to amplify rather than to correct those biases.[9] Deliberating groups have also been found to amplify, rather than to attenuate, reliance on the representativeness heuristic.[10] Such groups fall prey to even larger framing effects than individuals, so that when the same situation is described in different terms, groups are especially likely to be affected by the redescriptions.[11] Groups show more overconfidence than group members;[12]

they are even more affected by the biasing effect of bad arguments from lawyers.[13]

In an especially revealing finding, groups have been found to make more, rather than fewer, conjunction errors (believing that A and B are more likely to be true than A alone) than individuals when individual error rates are high—though fewer when individual error rates are low.[14] Groups do demonstrate a decreased level of reliance on the availability heuristic, but the decrease is slight, even when use of that heuristic leads to clear errors.[15]

Here's a disturbing finding, one with great relevance to group behavior in both politics and business: *Groups are more likely than individuals to escalate their commitment to a course of action that is failing—and all the more so if members identify strongly with the groups of which they are a part.*[16] There is a clue here about why companies, states, and even nations often continue with projects and plans that are clearly going awry. If a company is marketing a product that is selling poorly, it may well continue on its misguided course simply because of group dynamics. (Enron is a likely example.) So, too, with a nation whose economic policy or approach to foreign affairs is failing or hurting its citizens.

Why are individual cognitive errors so often amplified at the group level? Informational pressures and social influences are unquestionably at work. Suppose that most members of a group are prone to make certain errors. If the majority makes those errors, then most people will see others making the same errors. What they see will convey information about what is right. Those who are not specialists are likely to think: If most people make the same errors, maybe they are not errors at all. Social influences also play a role. If most group members make errors, others also might make them simply in order not to seem disagreeable or foolish. When groups do not correct the blunders of their members, this is a large reason.

To be sure, there is some evidence that deliberating groups can attenuate certain biases. Groups are especially likely to do better than the average individual when members are subject to *egocentric bias*, the bias that leads most of us to think that other people think and act as we do.[17] Most people believe that their tastes and preferences are typical. When asked what percentage of other people watch television on Saturday night, enjoy Bob Dylan, favor a particular political party, or believe that the latest Brad Pitt movie will win the Oscar, most of us show a bias in the direction that we ourselves favor. But in groups with diverse views, people quickly learn that their own position is not universally held, and hence the bias is reduced. In these cases, group deliberation supplies an important corrective.

Or consider the *hindsight bias*: people's tendency to believe, falsely but with the benefit of hindsight, that they would have accurately predicted the outcome of an event (an accident, a natural disaster, an illness, a change in the stock market). Compared to individuals, groups are slightly less susceptible to hindsight bias.[18] Apparently, group members who are not susceptible to that bias are able to persuade others that it is indeed a bias.

But the broader point is that with group discussion, individual errors are usually propagated rather than eliminated, and amplification of mistakes is quite likely. When individuals show a high degree of bias, groups are likely to be more biased, not less biased, than their median or average member.[19]

We have seen, from the Condorcet Jury Theorem, that as the size of the group expands, the likelihood of error from the group's majority expands toward 100 percent if each group member is more likely to be wrong than right. What I am emphasizing here is that social dynamics tend to aggravate rather than reduce the risk of group error. If this is so, then private organizations that engage in deliberation, as well as deliberators in legislatures and the executive branch, will be prone to error. Recall here the suggestion that both the CIA and NASA blundered because group processes failed to correct, and instead amplified, the initial biases internal to both agencies.

/ Hidden Profiles and Common Knowledge /

Suppose that group members have a lot of information, enough to produce the right outcome if that information is properly aggregated. Even if this is so, an obvious problem is that groups will not perform well if they emphasize shared information and slight information that is held by only one or a few members. The failure of the United States at the Bay of Pigs is a clear example, and the same problem infected the deliberating groups in Colorado. Countless studies demonstrate that this unfortunate result is highly likely.[20]

Hidden profiles has become the standard term for the accurate understandings that groups could obtain but do not. Suppose that individual group members, taken as a whole, have the information that could show that a particular political candidate is inferior or that a particular plan for environmental protection is best. But suppose, too, that the information that shows these things remains undisclosed because the group does not take account of it. In these circumstances, a hidden profile is involved. Hidden profiles are a clear failure of information aggregation, and they are all too common.

Hidden profiles are in turn a product of the *common knowledge effect*, through which information held by all group members has far more influence on group judgments than information held by only a few members.[21] The simple result is that groups are often unable to benefit from information that is limited to one or a few members (unless the one or the few are leaders, confident, or known to be experts). The most obvious explanation is the simple fact that, as a statistical matter, common knowledge is more likely to be communicated to the group; more people have that knowledge, and hence it is more likely to be repeated. But social influences play a role as well.

Examples /

Consider a simple demonstration of a hidden profile: a simulation of political elections. Information was parceled out to group members about three candidates for political office; if the information had been properly pooled, the group would have selected Candidate A, who was clearly the best choice.[22] The experiment involved two conditions. In the first condition, each member of the four-person group was given most of the relevant information (66 percent of the information about each candidate). In that condition, 67 percent of group members favored Candidate A before discussion, and 85 percent after discussion. This is a happy story of appropriate aggregation of information. Groups significantly outperformed individuals, apparently because of the exchange of information and reasons. Here, then, is an illustration of the possibility that groups can aggregate what members know in a way that produces sensible outcomes.

In the second condition, by contrast, the information that favored Candidate A was parceled out to various members of the group, rather than shared by all. As this condition was designed, the shared information favored the two unambiguously inferior candidates, B and C. If the unshared information emerged through discussion and was taken seriously, Candidate A would be chosen.

In that condition, fewer than 25 percent of group members favored Candidate A before discussion, a natural product of the initial distribution of information. But (and this is the key result) the number of people favoring Candidate A actually *fell* after discussion, simply because the shared information had disproportionate influence on group members. In other words, groups did worse, not better, than individuals when the key information was not initially shared by group members. The commonly held information was far more influential than the unshared information, to the detriment of the group's ultimate decision.

From this and many similar studies, the general conclusion is that when "the balance of unshared information opposes the initially most popular position . . . the unshared information will tend to be omitted from discussion and, therefore, will have little effect on members' preferences during group discussion."[23] That conclusion has a clear connection with the large-scale information failures at the CIA and similar failures at NASA. It follows that group decisions often reflect the initial preferences of group members even if the exchange of unshared information ought to have produced significant changes in people's opinions. Here, then, is an important source of failures by deliberating groups.

Nor does discussion increase the recall of unshared information. In the experiment just outlined, the major effect of discussion was to increase recall of the attributes of the initially most popular candidate. The disturbing conclusion is that when key information is unshared, groups are more likely to select a bad option after discussion than would their individual members before discussion.[24] So much, then, for the hope that deliberation will ensure healthy aggregations of opinion.

The Common Knowledge Effect /

These results are best understood as a consequence of the *common knowledge effect*, by which information held by all or most group members has the biggest influence on group judgments, far more than information held by one member or a few.[25] More precisely, the "influence of a particular item of information is directly and positively related to the number of group members who have knowledge of that item before the group discussion and judgment."[26] When information is unshared, group judgments have been found to be no more accurate than the average of the individual judgments, even though—and this is the central point— groups as a whole have far more information than do any of the individual members.[27]

In a key study, deliberating groups would have lost *nothing* in terms of accuracy if they had simply averaged the judgments of the people involved—a clear finding that deliberation may not improve on the judgments of statistical groups.[28] The more shared the information is (that is, the more that it stands as common knowledge), the more impact it will have on group members before discussion begins—and the more impact it will have as discussion proceeds, precisely because commonly held information is more likely to be discussed.

Most of the hidden profile experiments involve volunteer participants from college courses. Would the same results be found in the real world? Affirmative evidence comes from a hiring exercise involving high-level executives.[29] In this study, no experimenter controlled information about the various candidates. Instead, the executives' knowledge arose naturally from their own information searches. As a result of those searches, some information was known to all, some was partially shared, and some was uniquely held. Even with high-level executives, common information had a dispro-portionately large impact on discussions and conclusions. Disproportionately little weight was given to valuable information held by one person or a few.

The same study offers an additional finding of considerable importance. Some group members are "cognitively central,"[30] in the sense that their knowledge is shared with many other group members. What they know, other people know as well. A cognitively central group member is defined as one who possesses information in common with all or most group members. But other group members are "cognitively periph-eral," in the sense that their own information is uniquely held; what they know is known by no one else. Well-functioning groups need to take advantage of cognitively peripheral people. But it turns out that cognitively central people usually have a disproportionate influence in discussion, and they also show higher levels of participation in group deliberations. By contrast, cognitively peripheral people end up having little influence and do not much participate.

A simple explanation for these results is that group members prefer to hear information that is commonly held and prefer to hear people who have such information. Cognitively central people also have high levels of credibility; cognitively peripheral people have corresponding low levels. Indeed, the executives who were cognitively central ended up having a greater influence on the final report. The general conclusion is that when some group members count more than others, it is often because they know what everyone else knows. Unfortunately, more peripheral people, with unique knowledge, are sometimes the ones group members most need to hear.

As might be expected, a group's focus on shared informa-tion increases with the size of the group.[31] For this reason, many minds can go very badly wrong. In a study designed to test judgments about candidates for office, involving both three-person and six-person groups, all group discussions focused far more on shared information than on unshared information, but the effect was significantly greater for six-person groups. Most remarkably, "it was almost as likely for a shared item to be mentioned twice as it was for an unshared item to be mentioned at all."[32]

It follows that for very large groups—twelve people, thirty people, two hundred people, two million people—the effect of shared information will be compounded. And despite the failures of their deliberations, group members tend to be significantly more confident about their judgments after discussion—an especially alarming finding, because confidence and error are a bad combination.

Informational Influences and Social Pressures Again /
Why do hidden profiles remain hidden? The principal explanations build on the informational and social accounts emphasized in chapter 2. When information is held by all or most group members, it is especially likely, as a statistical matter, to be repeated in group discussion, and hence more likely to be influential than information that is held by one person or a few.[33] There are two different points here. First, information held by all or most group members is likely to influence individual judgments, and those judgments will in turn affect the judgments of the group.[34] Second, shared information, simply because it is shared, is more likely to be explored during group discussion.

Suppose that a team of five people is advising the president whether to embark on military action to combat a perceived threat to national security. If each of the five people has information indicating that the use of military force would be successful, that information is more likely to emerge in group discussion than are separate parcels of information, individually held by each advisor, suggesting that the use of force would run into trouble. If the team of advisors stresses the information that is held in advance by each, that information will have a disproportionate influence on the president's ultimate decision. This is a simple statistical point.

But hidden profiles remain significantly more hidden than would be predicted by statistics.[35] To understand the additional element, consider the finding that low-status members of groups are "increasingly reluctant over the course of discussion to repeat unique information."[36] Those in the group who are inexperienced or are thought to be low on the hierarchy are particularly loath to emphasize their privately held information as discussion proceeds.

This finding suggests that group members, especially lower-status ones, are nervous about emphasizing information that most group members lack. Indeed, lower-status members "are likely to drop unique information like a hot potato,"[37] partly because of the difficulty of establishing its credibility and relevance and partly because they risk the group's disapproval if they press a line of argument that others reject. Return here to the finding that cognitively peripheral members have little influence on the group. Those who have uniquely held information end up participating less than those who have shared information, and what they have to say is not much valued. In many deliberating groups, people who emphasize uniquely held information take an obvious social risk. And they know it.

This point creates a big problem for such groups, which will fail to get information that they need, and which can therefore be led to error. Consider the finding that group members typically *underestimate* the performance of low-status members and typically *overestimate* the performance of high-status members, in a way that gives high-status members a degree of deference that is not warranted by reality.[38]

In the same vein, those who discuss shared information obtain rewards in the form of an enhanced sense of competence in the eyes of others, and in their own eyes as well.[39] Strange but true: If someone tells you something you already know, you are apt to like that person, and yourself, a bit better as a result. In face-to-face discussions and in written tasks, people give higher ratings (in terms of knowledge, competence, and credibility) both to themselves and to others after receiving information that they knew already. It follows that someone with valuable, unshared information may best earn credibility "by telling others what they already know before telling them what they do not already know."[40] The general problem is that deliberating groups often perform poorly because they fail to elicit information that could steer them in the right directions.

/ Cascades and Polarization /

Informational Cascades /

Hidden profiles are closely related to *informational cascades*, which greatly impair group judgments. Cascades need not involve deliberation, but deliberative processes often involve cascades. As in the case of hidden profiles, the central point is that those involved in a cascade do not reveal what they know.

To see how informational cascades work, imagine a deliberating group that is deciding whether a company should market a proposed product.[41] Assume that the group members are announcing their views in sequence. From his or her own knowledge and experience, each member has some private information about what should be done. But each member also attends, reasonably enough, to the judgments of others. Andrews is the first to speak. He suggests that the product should indeed be marketed. Barnes now knows Andrews's judgment; it is clear that she, too, should certainly urge marketing the product if she agrees independently with Andrews. But if her independent judgment is otherwise, she would—if she trusts Andrews no more and no less than she trusts herself—be indifferent about what to do, and she might simply flip a coin.

Now turn to a third employee, Carlton. Suppose that both Andrews and Barnes have favored marketing the product, but that Carlton's own information, though not conclusive, suggests that this is a mistake. In that event, Carlton might well ignore what he knows and follow Andrews and Barnes. It is likely, after all, that both Andrews and Barnes had reasons for their conclusion, and unless Carlton thinks that his own information is better than theirs, he should follow their lead. If he does, Carlton is in a cascade.

Now suppose that Carlton is speaking in response to what Andrews and Barnes said, not on the basis of his own information, and also that subsequent deliberators know what Andrews, Barnes, and Carlton said. On reasonable assumptions, they will do exactly what Carlton did: favor the project regardless of their private information (which, we are supposing, is relevant but inconclusive). This will happen even if Andrews initially blundered. That initial blunder, in short, can start a process by which a number of people participate in creating serious mistakes.

If this is what is happening, there is a major social problem: People who are in the cascade do not disclose the information they privately hold. In the example just given, the company's decision will not reflect the overall knowledge, or the aggregate knowledge, of those within the company *even if the information held by individual employees, if actually revealed and aggregated, would produce a better and quite different result.* The reason for the problem is that individual employees are following the lead of those who came before.

Does all this seem unrealistic? Perhaps it does. But cascades do occur in the real world. Even among specialists, and indeed doctors, cascades are common. "Most doctors are not at the cutting edge of research; their inevitable reliance upon what colleagues have done and are doing leads to numerous surgical fads and treatment-caused illnesses."[42] Thus, an article in the *New England Journal of Medicine* explores "bandwagon diseases" in which doctors act like "lemmings, episodically and with a blind infectious enthusiasm pushing certain diseases and treatments primarily because everyone else is doing the same."[43] Some medical practices, including tonsillectomy, "seem to have been adopted initially based on weak information," and extreme differences in tonsillectomy frequencies (and other procedures) provide good evidence that cascades are at work.[44]

As another example, consider the existence of widely divergent group judgments about the origins and causes of AIDS, with some groups believing, falsely, that the first cases were observed in Africa as a result of sexual relations with monkeys, and with other groups believing, also falsely, that the virus was produced in government laboratories.[45] These and other views about AIDS are a product of social interactions and in particular of cascade effects. Deliberation often fails as a result.

Informational cascades create a big problem for those who are optimistic about group judgments. A mundane example: Suppose that on the game *Who Wants to Be a Millionaire?*, the audience is asked to say which character died in a movie based on the television show *Star Trek*. Suppose that the candidates are (a) Captain Kirk, (b) Mr. Spock, (c) Lieutenant Uhuru, and (d) Dr. McCoy. In a large audience, the plurality would almost certainly answer (b), which is correct. Those who do not know would divide themselves fairly randomly among the four options, and those who know would choose (b). Now suppose that several audience members vocally and confidently announced that they chose (a), and that they did so before the rest of the audience voted. Suppose, too, that audience members announced their votes publicly. Under plausible assumptions, the audience would select (a) in an informational cascade. If the discussion thus far is correct, such cascades can occur even when the stakes are much higher.

Reputational Cascades /
In a *reputational cascade*, people think they know what is right, or what is likely to be right, but they nonetheless go along with the crowd in order to maintain the good opinion of others. Suppose that Albert suggests that global warming is a serious problem, and that Barbara concurs with Albert, not because she actually thinks that Albert is right, but because she does not wish to seem to Albert to be ignorant or indifferent to environmental protection. If Albert and Barbara say that global warming is a serious problem, Cynthia might not contradict them publicly and might even appear to share their judgment, not because she believes that judgment to be correct, but because she does not want to face their hostility or lose their good opinion.

It should be easy to see how this process might generate a cascade. Once Albert, Barbara, and Cynthia offer a united front on the issue, their friend David might be reluctant to contradict them even if he thinks they are wrong. The apparently shared view of Albert, Barbara, and Cynthia carries information; that view might be right. But even if David has reason to believe that they are wrong, he might not want to take them on publicly. The problem, of course, is that the group will not hear what David knows.

In the actual world of group decisions, people are of course uncertain whether publicly expressed statements are a product of independent knowledge, participation in an informational cascade, or reputational pressure. Much of the time, listeners and observers probably overstate the extent to which the actions of others are based on independent information. Deliberating groups often fail as a result.

/ Group Polarization /

There are clear links among hidden profiles, social cascades, and the well-established phenomenon of group polarization, by which *members of a deliberating group typically end up in a more extreme position in line with their tendencies before deliberation began.*[46] Group polarization is a usual pattern with deliberating groups. It has been found in hundreds of studies in over a dozen countries.[47] The Colorado experiment, involving Boulder and Colorado Springs, was a case study in group polarization.

For example, those who disapprove of the United States and are suspicious of its intentions will increase their disapproval and suspicion if they exchange points of view. Indeed, there is specific evidence of this phenomenon among citizens of France: They dislike the United States a lot more, and trust the United States a lot less, after they talk with one another.[48] (In the aftermath of the 2003 U.S. invasion of Iraq, when french fries were relabeled "freedom fries," the citizens of the United States showed a similar pattern.) Group polarization provides a clue to the roots of extremism and even fanaticism and terrorism. All these can be fueled, not reduced, by deliberation.

Group polarization occurs for issues of fact as well as issues of value.[49] Group polarization has been found on obscure factual questions, such as how far Sodom (on the Dead Sea) is below sea level.[50] Or suppose that people are asked, on a bounded scale of zero to eight, how likely it is that a terrorist attack will occur in the United States in the next year, with zero indicating "zero probability," eight indicating "absolutely certain," seven indicating "overwhelmingly likely," six "more probable than not," and five "fifty-fifty." The answers from a deliberating group will tend to reveal group polarization, as the group's members move toward more extreme points on the scale, depending on their initial median point. If the predeliberation median is six, the group judgment will usually be seven; if the predeliberation median is three, the group judgment will usually be two.[51] Recall here that federal judges are highly susceptible to group polarization, as both Democratic and Republican appointees show far more ideological voting patterns when sitting with other judges appointed by a president of the same political party.[52] Juries polarize, too.[53]

Return here to the Colorado study, designed to explore political differences in the United States. Liberals polarized: When group members tended to support affirmative action, civil unions, and an international agreement to control global warming, they moved toward greater support after internal discussions. Conservatives polarized, too. There is an account here about how liberals and conservatives, and Democrats and Republicans, can move to extremes after speaking with, or at least listening to, one another.

Why does group polarization occur? There are several reasons.[54] The first and most important involves informational influences. Fortunately, most people listen to the arguments made by other people. In any group with some initial inclination, the views of most people in the group will inevitably be skewed in the direction of that inclination. Suppose that the majority position within a group is that global warming is a serious problem or that the incumbent president is doing a terrific job. As a statistical matter, the arguments favoring that initial position will be more numerous than the arguments pointing in the other direction. Individuals will have heard of some, but not all, of the arguments that emerge from group deliberation. As a result of hearing the various arguments, deliberation will lead people toward a more extreme point in line with what group members initially believed. Through this process, many minds can polarize, and in exactly the same direction.

Consider the fact that extremists and terrorists hear a sharply limited number of arguments, all pointing in the same direction. When people of different political stripes polarize in democratic nations, including the United States, informational influences play a key role.

The second explanation involves social influences. People usually want to be perceived favorably by other group members. Sometimes people's publicly stated views are, to a greater or lesser extent, a function of how they want to present themselves. Once they hear what others believe, some will adjust their positions at least slightly in the direction of the dominant position. In a left-wing group, for example, those who lean to the left will be more acceptable, and for this reason they might well end up leaning somewhat more to the left. There is a particular problem here. When people are in the presence of political authorities—

senators, governors, presidents—they often shift their public views so as to conform with the views of those authorities. For this reason, leaders often do not hear what they need to know, because so many minds silence themselves. A mass of people can have the same silencing effect as leaders, thus leading deliberative processes to fail.

The third explanation of group polarization stresses the close links among confidence, extremism, and corroboration by others.[55] As people gain confidence, they usually become more extreme in their beliefs. Agreement from others tends to increase confidence, and for this reason like-minded people, having deliberated with one another, become more sure that they are right and thus more extreme. In many contexts, people's opinions become more extreme simply because their views have been corroborated, and because they become more confident after learning that others share their views.[56] Many minds can badly blunder in this way.

A great deal of work suggests that group polarization is heightened when people have a sense of shared identity, and this point helps to suggest yet another explanation of polarization.[57] People may polarize because they are attempting to conform to the position they see as typical within their own group. If their group's identity is made especially salient, the in-group norms are likely to become more extreme.[58] In the Colorado experiment, many groups were all the more prone to polarization when their discussions referred to some group with whom they disagreed, such as "the liberals." Democrats and Republicans often become more sharply separated for the same reason.

There is a further point: If arguments come from a member of an in-group, they are especially likely to be persuasive. Such arguments are more likely to seem right. It is also reasonable to think that people would fear the social pressures that come from rejecting what an in-group member has to say. By contrast, the views of out-group members have far less force and might even be irrelevant.[59] Should you really listen to someone who belongs to a group that you believe to be systematically and egregiously wrong? Will a member of Hamas much care about the policy commitments of a citizen of Israel? The reputational pressure will also be reduced: Do you really have to worry about rejecting the views of someone usually thought to be wrong by people like you? If a self-identified conservative hears arguments from someone who is known to be left of center, those arguments might well fall on deaf ears. The clear lesson is that when a group is highly cohesive, and when its members are closely identified with it, polarization is especially likely—and likely to be especially large.

Does group polarization lead to accurate or inaccurate answers? Do deliberating groups err when they polarize? No general answer would make sense. Everything depends on the relationship between the correct answer and the group's predeliberation tendencies. If the group is leaning toward the right answer, polarization might lead them directly to the truth. But there are no guarantees here. As a result of the relevant influences, some people will fail to disclose what they know. When individuals are leaning in a direction that is mistaken, the mistake will be amplified by group deliberation. We have already encountered an example: When most people are prone to make logical errors, group processes lead to more errors rather than fewer. The same is true when jury members are biased as a result of pretrial publicity; the jury as a group becomes more biased than individual jurors were.[60] This is polarization in action, and it produces large blunders.

Polarization, the Internet, and the Daily Me /
What is the effect of new technologies on polarization?
There is no simple answer here. Many people are using the
Internet to encounter new perspectives. They may live in an
information cocoon—their workplace, their school, their
neighborhood—and the Internet can greatly broaden their
horizons. Cocoons and echo chambers, emerging from
simple geography, are easy to escape with just a few seconds
on a few Web sites. In this sense, curious people can obtain
remarkable aggregations of information without leaving
their screens. Many citizens, in isolated areas or isolated
nations, escape their confines, and learn an extraordinary
amount, simply by virtue of the Internet.

But recall the Daily Me, the prophecy of a personalized
communications universe, in which you consult only those
topics and opinions that you like. Because of the possibility of
personalization, people can construct "profiles" that include
what they accept and exclude what they reject. To the extent
that this happens, polarization is all the more probable, as
like-minded people sort themselves into virtual communities
that seem comfortable and comforting. Instead of good
information aggregation, bad polarization is the outcome.[61]

In fact, the best search engines, including Google, offer an
intriguingly mixed picture here. The good news is that
search engines turn up an extraordinary range of material,
often with varied and competing perspectives. This indeed is
the most important part of the story. But there is less good
news, and it is also important: Some searches produce the
same set of opinions, not diversity. Indeed, personalized
searches, which are now possible, ensure that Google can
give you the kinds of things in which you, in particular,
have previously shown an interest. It follows that with

personalized searches, different people with their different histories will automatically receive different answers to exactly the same searches. In terms of convenience and usefulness, this is a great benefit. But in terms of information aggregation, it has an unfortunate side.

Right and Wrong: Group Judgments and Nonfactual Questions /

My emphasis thus far has been on questions with demonstrably correct answers, above all disputed issues of fact. But groups are often asked to answer questions that are not purely factual. Issues involving morality, politics, and law require judgments of value, not merely fact. Is preemptive war morally permissible? Should more money be redistributed from the wealthy to the poor? Should the minimum wage be increased? Should capital punishment be permitted? Should same-sex marriages be allowed? When, if ever, is theft morally acceptable?

When people answer such questions, informational influences and social pressures will almost inevitably play a major role. The phenomena discussed here have clear analogues in the domain of politics and morality. Group polarization has been found with respect to moral outrage: When individual jurors are outraged about corporate misconduct, deliberation leads juries to become more outraged still.[62] If outraged people get together, they are likely to end up more outraged than they were when they first started to talk. Political hatred, and acts of violence, often are produced in this way. As we saw in the Colorado experiment, group discussion frequently produces polarization on moral and political issues.[63]

There is every reason to think that cascade effects occur for issues of politics and morality. Suppose that people are asking whether a politician would make a good nominee for high office. Informational cascades are highly likely; indeed, an informational cascade helped to account for the Democratic nomination of John Kerry in 2004.[64] When Democrats shifted from Howard Dean to John Kerry in that year, it was not because each Democratic voter made an independent judgment on Kerry's behalf. It was in large part because of a widespread perception that other people were flocking to Kerry. Duncan Watts's amusing account is worth quoting at length:

> A few weeks before the Iowa caucuses, Kerry's campaign seemed dead, but then he unexpectedly won Iowa, then New Hampshire, and then primary after primary. How did this happen? . . . When everyone is looking to someone else for an opinion—trying, for example, to pick the Democratic candidate they think everyone else will pick—it's possible that whatever information other people might have gets lost, and instead we get a cascade of imitation that, like a stampeding herd, can start for no apparent reason and subsequently go in any direction with equal likelihood. Stock market bubbles and cultural fads are the examples that most people associate with cascades . . . but the same dynamics can show up even in the serious business of Democratic primaries. . . . We think of ourselves as autonomous individuals, each driven by [our] own internal abilities and desires and therefore solely responsible for our own behavior, particularly when it comes to voting. No voter ever admits—even to herself—that she chose Kerry because he won New Hampshire.[65]

Cascades can be found for many contested political questions, including the legitimacy of affirmative action, abortion, preemptive war, and capital punishment. Perspectives on environmental and economic issues are often a product of cascade effects. Few of us have thought long and hard about these questions. We often end up thinking what we think others think, at least if we think that those others think as we do. When "political correctness" moves people to the left or to the right, cascades are typically involved. These points raise a warning flag about any situation in which citizens sort themselves into communities of like-minded others. In such communities, cascades are almost inevitable, and they might well be based on poor thinking and confusion. The problem is that the same forces that produce factual errors operate in the moral and political domains as well.

It is in those domains, above all, that groups end up at a more extreme point in line with their predeliberation tendencies. Suppose that citizens of Iran tend to distrust the United States and its intentions with respect to the "war on terror." After they have spoken with one another, their distrust is likely to grow. Or suppose that a group of Americans approve of the incumbent president and believe that in domestic as well as foreign affairs, his decisions tend to be good. Their internal discussions are likely to lead them to think that his decisions are great, not merely good.

If facts are not involved, we may not be able to be so confident that any particular profile is hidden. But hidden profiles occur for values as well as for facts, in a way that can much damage deliberation. If one perspective is widely held within the group, and if other relevant perspectives are dispersed, the widely held perspective will end up dominating the dispersed ones. Suppose that the group consists of six men and one woman, and that the topic is sexual harassment. If the woman in the group knows something that none of the men knows, the men are unlikely to learn what she knows, and their shared knowledge, or beliefs, will dominate. Or suppose that every group member knows one reason that argues against capital punishment, but that several other factors, arguing in favor of capital punishment, are widely dispersed among group members. We can safely assume that the common knowledge will have a much larger effect. Surely there is a big problem if certain views are not taken into account in group deliberation simply because those views are dispersed within the group.

It might be controversial to suggest that groups amplify individual errors in the moral, political, and legal domains, because in those domains, we might not be able to say with confidence that one or another view counts as an "error." Skeptics about morality, politics, and law, rejecting the view that the underlying questions have correct answers, would insist that any shifts introduced by deliberation cannot be said to be right or wrong. But genuine skepticism is extremely hard to defend.[66] Without engaging the philosophical issues, we can simply note that many different views about the nature of morality acknowledge the possibility of individual error—and that if individual error does occur, group error will occur as well. As obvious examples, consider the persistence of slavery and racial segregation.

For moral, political, and legal questions, the argument on behalf of group deliberation is not fundamentally different from what it is for factual questions.[67] Unless we are skeptics, we will agree that one point of deliberation is to ensure that these questions are correctly answered—that is, are answered by reference to good reasons, even if we disagree about what they are. And if this is so, then there is strong reason to be concerned, for political, moral, and legal questions no less than factual ones, that group judgments will be impaired by the mechanisms I have traced here.

A more general lesson follows. I have said that many people have celebrated deliberative conceptions of democracy, largely with the thought that deliberative processes among diverse people are likely to lead participants in better or more sensible directions. The underlying judgment is easy to understand. Diverse perspectives can ensure that people see far more than they saw before. But we can now understand that even under ideal conditions, emphasized by proponents of deliberation, group members can be led to err, not despite deliberation but because of it. When members of a religious community end up entrenched in their belief in, say, traditional gender roles, or when members of a liberal group end up still more committed to a highly progressive income tax, social dynamics, leaving hidden profiles, may well be responsible. The fact that deliberation increases both confidence and uniformity will leave the strong but potentially misleading impression that deliberation has produced sense rather than nonsense.

Can anything be done? Is it possible to take steps to make deliberation work better? I believe that it is. But to see how, and even why, we have to venture a bit afield. We have to look at markets rather than deliberation. We have to move from the old to the new. We have to investigate some creative and fresh mechanisms for aggregating information from many minds. Some of the most promising of those mechanisms involve the Internet.

Chapter Four / **Money, Prices, and Prediction Markets**

Statistical groups elicit and incorporate the views of group members. Deliberating groups are supposed to do the same. A very different way to aggregate information is to rely on prices and on the signals that prices give.

To see why that method might work, consider the familiar informal challenge when people disagree on some question: "Want to bet?" The point of the challenge is to suggest that the speaker is really confident of her judgment, enough so as to ask the person with whom she disagrees to back her conviction with money. Much of the time, the challenge is successful in the sense that it operates to establish to all concerned that one or another belief is weakly held. When people ask for a bet, they are bypassing deliberation and offering a good clue about the confidence with which they hold their views. But if we want to get access to many minds, we might see if economic incentives can be used far more formally and systematically.

In fact, that is exactly what markets do. What is the source of the prices of soap, cereals, shoes, and computers? In a market economy, we don't decide on prices by polling people and taking the median answer. We don't ask people to deliberate about prices and choose the ones that make the best sense. Nor do prices emerge from any judgment by experts. (The Soviet Union tried that.) Instead, prices are a product of the independent judgments of many people, each with his own dispersed beliefs, judgments, and tastes. Of course, markets are very far from perfect, and I devote some discussion to their errors, which can be egregious; but much of the time, they do an excellent job in aggregating privately held information.

Suppose that we are inclined to celebrate the information-aggregating properties of markets. If so, it would seem plain that if we are attempting to improve on the answers produced by statistical averages and deliberating groups, we might consider an increasingly popular possibility: *Create a market.*[1] Prediction markets, in some ways a recent innovation, have proved remarkably successful at forecasting future events. They do far better, in some domains, than deliberating groups. Such markets are worth sustained attention, in part because they offer important lessons about how to make deliberation go better or worse, and in part because they provide a useful model for any private and public organization that seeks access to many minds. Prediction market theorist Robin Hanson has, in fact, coined the term "futarchy" for a system in which such markets play a large role in governmental decisions.[2]

A central advantage of prediction markets is that they give people the right incentive to disclose the information they hold. People stand to win money if they get it right and to lose money if they get it wrong. Recall that in a deliberating group, members may have little incentive to say what they know. By speaking out, they provide benefits to others, while possibly facing high private costs. Prediction markets realign incentives in a way that is precisely designed to overcome these problems. People can capture, rather than give to others, the benefits of disclosure. Because investments in such markets are generally not revealed to the public, investors need not fear that their reputation will be at risk if, for example, they have predicted that a company's sales will be low or that a certain candidate will be elected president.

With prediction markets, the use of private information will be reflected in prices. Suppose that a prediction market suggests that it is likely that intelligent extraterrestrial life will be discovered within the next year. Suppose that for a $100 bet, you can receive $200 if you predict that no such discovery will be made. This market's prediction is preposterous (I speculate!), and skeptics are likely to make money if they are willing to bet otherwise. (Want to bet?) Of course, many prediction markets raise harder questions. The key point is that those with specialized information can gamble as they see fit. People who do not want to participate, because they have no idea what to predict, have every incentive to stand aside. To be sure, some people might refuse to participate, not because they lack information, but because they lack the money to gamble. But at least it can be said that such markets give people a powerful incentive to reveal what they know.

In these crucial ways, prediction markets have large advantages over surveys. Suppose that the question is how many children I have. A survey of numerous people is far less likely to produce the right answer than a market, in which informed people can make money. What is true for mundane or personal questions is true for larger questions as well, including the likelihood of natural disasters, changes in the economy, the outcome of an election, and the success of a movie.

Recall that under the Condorcet Jury Theorem, the average vote of a large group will be wrong if most group members are likely to err. In a prediction market, the existence of incentives greatly increases the likelihood that each investor will prove to be right. Those without information will not participate; those with a lot of information will participate a great deal. Crucially, the problems that infect deliberating groups are reduced in prediction markets. As a result, such markets have often proved remarkably accurate. Perhaps most important, prediction markets have been found not to amplify individual errors but to eliminate them; the prices that result from trading prove reliable even if many individual traders err. Because of their accuracy, prediction markets are receiving a great deal of attention in the private sector, as we shall see, and it is easy to find software and services to support their use.[3]

Of course, investors, like everyone else, are subject to cognitive biases and to the informational pressure imposed by the views of others. Markets have their own fads and fashions, and prices can be way off. But a market creates strong incentives for revelation of whatever information people actually hold. A profile may remain hidden in a deliberating group, but in a market, those with hidden information, uniquely held, are in a position to make a lot of money—and they are likely to exploit the opportunity. For small groups, of course, prediction markets are likely to be too "thin" to be useful; a certain number of investors is required to get a market off the ground.[4] In many contexts, however, private and public organizations might use markets as a complement to or even a substitute for deliberation. They might create markets, or watch markets, when they are deciding what to do.

Let us now turn to actual practice.

/ Practice and Evidence /

An Abandoned Initiative /
In many imaginable markets, people might make claims about facts or predictions about the future, and they might

stand to gain or lose from their predictions. In the summer
of 2003, analysts at the Department of Defense built directly
on this idea.[5] To predict important events in the world,
including terrorist attacks, they sought to create a kind of
market in which ordinary people could actually place bets.
The proposed Policy Analysis Market would have allowed
people to invest in their predictions about such matters as
the growth of the Egyptian economy, the gross domestic
product of the United States, the likelihood of a bioweapons
attack on Israel, the overthrow of the king of Jordan, the
death of national leaders, the military withdrawal of the
United States from specified nations, and the likelihood of
terrorist attacks in the United States. Investors would have
won or lost money on the basis of the accuracy of their
predictions.

Predictably, the Policy Analysis Market produced a storm
of criticism. Ridiculed as "offensive" and "useless," the
proposal was abandoned. Senator Tom Daschle called the
market "the most irresponsible, outrageous and poorly
thought-out of anything that I have heard the administration propose to date."[6] Senator Byron Dorgan argued that it
is "morally bankrupt for a government agency to make a
profitable game out of the deaths of American troops, heads
of state, and nuclear missile attacks."[7] A private Policy
Analysis Market, specializing in the Middle East, was
promised in 2003, but it did not go forward.[8] Nonetheless,
several such markets, asking for predictions about national
and international events, are now in place. In fact, they are
flourishing on the Internet.

Amid the war on terrorism, why was the Department of
Defense so interested in the Policy Analysis Market? The
answer is simple: It wanted to have some assistance in
predicting geopolitical events, including those that would

endanger U.S. interests, and it believed that a market would provide that help. It speculated that if many minds could be given an incentive to aggregate their private information, in the way that the Policy Analysis Market would do, government officials would learn a great deal. Apparently it believed that such a market would provide an important supplement to deliberative processes both within and without government. No one knows how the Department of Defense would have reacted to the projections of prediction markets; the most reasonable speculation is that those projections would have been used, not as the final word, but as providing valuable information about future events. And although the Policy Analysis Market was not really a market in terrorism futures, one of its designers has argued that such futures are technically feasible—and might well be helpful.[9]

In recent years, prediction markets have done more than provide valuable information. In countless domains, their forecasts have proved extremely accurate.[10]

Iowa Electronic Markets /

Since 1988, the University of Iowa has run the Iowa Electronic Markets (IEM), which allow people to bet on the outcome of presidential elections. The system has evolved over time. Originally, the IEM permitted people to trade only in the expected fraction of the popular vote to be obtained by presidential candidates.[11] Securities were offered that would pay $2.50 multiplied by the specified candidate's share of the vote. If, for example, George H. W. Bush received 50 percent of the vote, the shareholder would receive $1.25. Shares could be bought and sold until the day before the election.

The IEM have greatly expanded from these modest roots. Traders have been able to bet on the market capitalization that Google will achieve in its initial public offering, the price of Microsoft stock at a future date, and Federal Reserve monetary policy, in addition to the outcomes of a range of U.S. elections.[12]

For presidential elections—still the most popular markets that IEM operate—traders have recently been permitted to choose from two types of markets. In the "winner-take-all" market, traders win $1 for each "future" in the winning candidate that they own; they receive nothing for shares of the losing candidate. In a "vote-share" market, traders in "candidate futures" win $1 multiplied by the proportion of the popular vote that the candidate receives. Thus, in a winner-take-all market, a "Dukakis future" was worth nothing after the election, whereas in a vote-share market, each Dukakis future paid $0.456.

In a winner-take-all market, the market price reflects traders' perceptions of the likelihood that each candidate will win the election. More interestingly, observers can use the prices in a vote-share market much as they might use a poll. In each case, the market price reflects the aggregate information held by participants, offering a "prediction" about the likely outcome.

The IEM operate much like an ordinary stock market. To enter, each participant must purchase "unit portfolios" consisting of one future in each candidate for each dollar the trader puts into the market. Once traders have bought enough of these unit portfolios, they can unbundle the contracts and trade individual shares. All trading is fully computerized, and traders must reach the markets through the Internet. As in a typical stock market, traders can issue bids and asks or simply accept outstanding offers. Most traders merely accept offers rather than choosing their own prices, but a small group of "marginal traders" trade frequently and post their own proposed trades. As we shall see, it is these traders who have the greatest effect on prices.

As a predictor, the IEM have produced highly accurate judgments. Before the 2004 elections, they did far better than professional polling organizations,[13] outperforming polls 451 out of 596 times.[14] In the week before the four elections from 1988 to 2000, the predictions in the Iowa market showed an average absolute error of just 1.5 percentage points, a significant improvement over the 2.1 percentage point error in the final Gallup polls.[15] In 2004, the Iowa market did even better. On midnight of November 1, it showed Bush with 50.45 percent of the vote and Kerry with 49.55 percent, very close to the final numbers of 51.56 percent for Bush and 48.44 percent for Kerry.[16] This prediction was far better than the predictions that emerged from the more conventional indicators of likely results, including consumer confidence and job growth.[17] Notably, the IEM have proved accurate not only on election eve but also in long forecasting horizons.[18] Professional polls ask people for their anticipated vote, not for their judgment about the likely winner; it is striking that answers to the latter question, posed with an economic incentive, outperform answers to the former.

Prediction markets are hardly limited to the United States. In other nations, universities are operating similar markets; examples include the University of British Columbia Election Stock Market, involving Canadian elections, and the Vienna University of Technology, operating the Austrian Electronic Market. Although the relevant districts are quite small, Australian bookmakers have shown a high degree of accuracy in predicting district-level races.[19]

InTrade, a political market based in Dublin, accurately predicted not only the 2004 victory for President Bush but also the particular outcomes in the battleground states.[20]

Other Prediction Markets: Hollywood, Weather, Google, Microsoft, and Beyond /

Prediction markets, aggregating the views of many minds, are flourishing outside the political domain. Consider the Hollywood Stock Exchange (HSX), in which people predict (among other things) Oscar nominees and winners as well as opening weekend box office figures. The level of accuracy has been extremely impressive, especially in view of the fact that the traders use virtual rather than real money. HSX has often offered accurate predictions of a movie's gross receipts before release; its predictions are even better after opening weekend.[21] As a result, studios are relying on HSX estimates in making decisions about the distribution of their films.[22]

HSX has also proved successful in predicting award winners. Among its most impressive achievements to date is its uncanny accuracy in predicting Oscar winners in 2005, with correct judgments in all eight of the categories for which trading was allowed. An interesting counterpoint: Tradesports.com, a prediction market that uses real rather than virtual money, predicted only six of eight Oscar winners in that year. In fact, prediction markets that use virtual money have been found, in many circumstances, to do as well as markets that rely on real money.[23]

When entertainment and law meet, prediction markets do well. Days before the ultimate verdict in the Michael Jackson case, insiders knew what would happen. As one reporter noted in advance, "Whether or not Michael Jackson's jurors still have a reasonable doubt about his guilt, the wild world of Internet betting has rendered judgment: the smart money is on acquittal."[24] Many people believe that "you can't predict the weather," but the National Weather Service does quite well, and orange juice futures do even better.[25] The markets for the demand for gas outperform the experts on the demand for gas.[26] A large prediction market focuses on the likelihood that economic data released later in the week will show specific values;[27] the market has performed at least as well as the consensus forecasts of a survey of about fifty professional forecasters.

Betting markets do extremely well in predicting the outcomes of horse races—far better, in fact, than experts.[28] Of course, most gamblers on horse races lose money and leave unhappy, but consider this: The favorites finish first more often than in any other position, the second-ranked horses finish second more often than in any other position, the third-ranked horses finish third, and so on.[29] More generally, online sports betting markets do quite well in predicting actual outcomes.[30]

As I have noted, companies are using prediction markets, too. Hewlett Packard (HP) and the California Institute of Technology initiated a project to study prediction markets as an information aggregation mechanism involving product sales.[31] The experimenters selected people who worked in different parts of HP's business operation. Because of its small size, the market was a very "thin" one, meaning that there were few participants, and hence the market was far less liquid than the much "thicker" IEM. Participants were chosen with the belief that each could contribute information from his department.

The markets were organized so that securities existed for intervals of sales. For example, one security would pay off if sales were between one and ten printers; another would pay off if sales were between ten and twenty. In most of the experiments, the possible range of sales was divided into ten intervals of equal size. On the basis of the prices of each security, the experimenters could guess how many units HP would sell that month. Prediction markets were expected to have large advantages over internal projections that involve deliberation. Employees involved in sales have an incentive to understate projected outcomes to ensure that they do not fall short of expectations; this bias, or a competing bias in favor of excessive optimism, might well be reduced through market incentives.

The results showed that the markets' predictions were a considerable improvement over HP's official forecasts. In no fewer than six of the eight markets for which official forecasts were available, the market prediction was significantly closer to the actual outcome than the official forecast was.

For its part, Google has created a large set of prediction markets to help forecast its own development.[32] The relevant markets predict launch dates for products, new office openings, and a range of other outcomes of importance to the company. As of September 2005, more than a thousand Google employees had bid on 146 events. People did not invest real money, but the virtual money used for the markets could be redeemed for various prizes, including seven large cash prizes per quarter. The larger prizes were given out through a drawing; users with more virtual money had more tickets in the drawing and therefore a better chance of winning. Smaller prizes (gift certificates and T-shirts) were given to the top one hundred or so winners, so that if an employee invested well, he received something, even if not a large cash prize.

Consider a partial list of Google's markets in 2005, which include fun predictions as well as those relating to the business:

2nd Quarter, 2005 (April–June)

Total 30-day active Gmail users
Total 30-day active Google groups
Number of new full-time engineering offer accepts
Number of new full-time offer accepts
Number of Web pages indexed
Total 1-month active Orkut users
China engineering office opens?
Will [secret product] launch?
Will the U.S. average gas price reach $2.50 by June 30?
Number of 7-day active [prediction market] users on
    May 1?
Will Episode III of *Star Wars* have a good rating?
    (Outcome determined by RottenTomatoes.com
    rating)

3rd Quarter, 2005 (July–September)

Russia engineering office opens?
Will Google open an Israel office?
Number of wireless pageviews
U.S. average gas price on Sept. 26, 2005
Will John Roberts be confirmed for U.S. Supreme
    Court?
Will the U.S. average gas price reach $3.00 by Sept. 30?
If the market "New Hires in Q305" is run, will it
    attract interest? (This market was an attempt to use
    markets to determine which markets would be
    popular.)

4th Quarter, 2005 (October–December)

Number of new machines released in Nov. 2005
How many people will RSVP to the MV holiday party?

Will Google print reach [a certain number of] books
   live in the index?
Number of 30-day active Gmail users
[X million] iGoogle users by end of quarter?
Will Google get the WiFi contract in SF?
Will London engineering office open?
Will [secret product] launch?
Number of wireless pageviews
Will a [secret product and partnership] be announced
   by Q106?
Will Brad Pitt and Angelina Jolie get married during
   2005?
Will Harriet Miers be confirmed to U.S. Supreme
   Court?
Will the U.S. average gas price reach $3.00 by Dec. 27?

The outcomes have been quite accurate, with prices
generally representing real probabilities. According to Bo
Cowgill, the project manager, "If we look at all events that
we said were 80% likely, 80% of them should come true and
20% should fail. If we look at all events that we said were
70% likely, 70% of them should come true and 30% should
not. This correlation is roughly what we've seen actually
happening." In addition, the results proved extremely
helpful to the company. In Cowgill's words, "We also found
that the market prices gave decisive, informative predictions
in the sense that their predictive power increased as time
passed and uncertainty was resolved."[33] Apparently, dispersed
knowledge within the company has been accurately aggregated in this way.

Did Google's prices really represent probabilities? For
some people, a picture is worth a thousand words; it is
therefore worthwhile to consider the graph in Figure 4.1. The

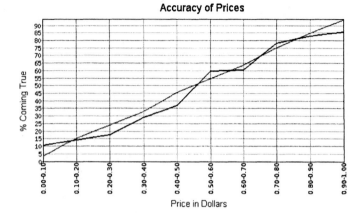

Accuracy of Prices

Price in Dollars

Figure 4.1

straighter line represents the average price, reflecting a judgment about how often outcomes in that group should occur according to the markets. The more curvy line represents how often the predicted outcomes actually did occur. As Cowgill writes, "Ideally these would be equal, and as you can see they're pretty close. So our prices really do represent probabilities—very exciting!"[34]

Microsoft, too, has been making good use of prediction markets. In 2004, pilot markets were introduced, including an evaluation of how many robotic cars would finish the DARPA Grand Challenge race. The market accurately predicted the number, which was zero. For an especially revealing episode, consider Microsoft's very first internal market. In August 2004, a prediction market was created to forecast the release date for a software project. (The product was an internal tool, not one that Microsoft sells.) The official release date was November, three months away; high-level management was confident that the release date would be met. In mid-August, the market was opened to twenty-five employee traders, each staked by Microsoft with $50 to trade. Their "securities" were pre-November, November, December, January, February, and after February. Within three minutes of the beginning of trading, November was selling for a price consistent with a 1.2 percent chance of meeting the release date, a figure that rose only slightly, to 3 percent, over the next twenty-four hours. Surprised by these numbers, the project's director investigated, concluded that the schedule was in fact unrealistic, and made a number of changes. (The product was released the last week in February.)

More recently, Microsoft has run a number of prediction markets, involving schedules (when products will reach specified milestones), revenues and profits, and defects (how many bugs of a certain kind or severity will be reported in a specified time). To avoid gambling laws, Microsoft funds the markets; participants do not risk their own money. But the company provides cash prizes to traders owning the right securities, and traders are permitted to enter a lottery with raffle tickets in proportion to the accuracy of their predictions. (I am told that Xbox game consoles are very popular prizes!)

To date, the markets are doing well in predicting outcomes, at least in the sense that when a security for an event is highly priced, the event is likely to come to pass. A surprise: One of the primary advantages of the prediction markets, to management, has been to provide information about potential divisions between the "crowd," as reflected in the price, and the senior managers. A possible reaction is that in the face of such divisions, either the market is right, or the manager is right; in either case, it is important to reach a better understanding. Google and Microsoft are hardly the only companies that have used prediction markets; Eli Lilly, Goldman Sachs, Deutsche Bank, and Hewlett Packard have also done so, and the number is rapidly growing.

In the United States, legal prohibitions restrict futures trading, but numerous off-shores sites are easy to find, and several onshore markets have managed to operate within legal limits, sometimes by using "play" or "virtual" money, sometimes with cash. Around the same time as the disaster produced by Hurricane Katrina in 2005, a hurricane futures market developed (http://hurricanefutures.miami.edu/), permitting invitation-only trades among specialists, allowing investments of $5 to $500. The goal is to predict where a given hurricane will land. Using play money, the Tech Buzz Game (http://buzz.research.yahoo.com/bk/index.html) asks people to predict the future popularity of various technologies. Its asserted goal is to invoke crowd wisdom to make forecasts. (As of this writing, iPod Video is expected to do particularly well.)

We can easily find actual or proposed prediction markets about any number of questions: Will gas prices reach a specified level? Will the United States attack Iran? Will cellular life be found on Mars? Will Osama bin Laden be captured by a certain date? Will smallpox return to the United States? Will there be a sequel to certain movies (*Pride and Prejudice II, Star Wars VII*)? Will the Federal Communications Commission be abolished? These and many more questions have been asked on prediction markets; the number grows every day.

Hayek's Marvel /

All in all, prediction markets have been quite successful in terms of the aggregate accuracy of the resulting "prices." Why is this? The best place to start is with Friedrich Hayek, the great twentieth-century critic of socialism and economic planning. Throughout his life, Hayek was concerned with how to obtain dispersed information. His emphasis was on markets rather than on deliberation, to which he devoted no attention.

Hayek's most important contribution to social thought is captured in his short 1945 paper, "The Use of Knowledge in Society."[35] Hayek claims that the great advantage of prices is that they aggregate both the information and the tastes of numerous people, incorporating far more material than could possibly be assembled by any central planner or board. He emphasizes the unshared nature of information, the "dispersed bits of incomplete and frequently contradictory knowledge which all the separate individuals possess."[36] That knowledge certainly includes facts about products, but it also includes preferences and tastes, and all of these must be taken into account by a well-functioning market. Hayek stresses above all the "very important but unorganized knowledge which cannot possibly be called scientific in the sense of general rules: the knowledge of the particular circumstances of time and place."[37]

For Hayek, the key economic question is how to incorporate that unorganized and dispersed knowledge. That problem cannot possibly be solved by any particular person or board. Central planners cannot have access to all of the knowledge held by particular people. Taken as a whole, the knowledge held by those people is far greater than that held by even the most well-chosen experts. Recall here Aristotle's claims about deliberating groups: When diverse groups "all come together . . . they may surpass—collectively and as a body, although not individually—the quality of the few best. . . . Some appreciate one part, some another, and all together appreciate all."[38] Hayek's argument is that, whether or not Aristotle was right about deliberation, the possibility of surpassing the quality of the few best certainly does hold for free markets.

Hayek adds here a point about the immense importance of change as such. Economic planners typically underrate the need for frequent changes in prices and output. Even economists neglect the constant little changes that constitute the whole economic picture. But society must find some way to make the necessary adaptations as conditions shift. No expert or deliberating group can anticipate all relevant changes; those changes are too numerous and too small. Sensible decisions must be a product of some kind of decentralized process, one that incorporates many minds. What might that process look like?

Here Hayek offers his central point: The best solution comes from the price system. In a system in which knowledge of relevant facts is dispersed among many people, prices act as an astonishingly concise and accurate coordinating and signaling device. They incorporate that dispersed knowledge and in a sense also publicize it, because the price itself operates as a signal to all.

Equally important, the price system has a wonderfully automatic quality, particularly in its capacity to respond to change. If fresh information shows that a product—a television, a car, a watch—doesn't always work, people's demand for it will rapidly fall, and so, too, the price. And when a commodity suddenly becomes more scarce, its users must respond to that fact. The market works remarkably well as a whole, not because any participant can see all its features, but because the relevant information is communicated to everyone through prices.

Hayek claims that it "is more than a metaphor to describe the price system as a kind of machinery for registering changes, or a system of telecommunications which enables individual producers to watch merely the movement of a few pointers."[39] Hayek describes this process as a "marvel," and adds that he has chosen that word on purpose so as "to shock the reader out of the complacency with which we often take the working of the mechanism for granted."[40]

Hayek believes that this marvel has analogies in "nearly all truly social phenomena, with language and with most of our cultural inheritance. . . . We make constant use of formulas, symbols, and rules whose meaning we do not understand and through the use of which we avail ourselves of the assistance of knowledge which individually we do not possess."[41] Language and culture itself are produced not by a single mind but by widely dispersed people with their own bits of information, producing goods from which all of us can benefit. And each of these evolves rapidly over time, incorporating and discarding material as human communities organize themselves.

Whenever a system creates a price, and many people participate in creating that price, Hayek's arguments are available. We can see a link not only between Aristotle and Hayek but also between Hayek's view and the Condorcet Jury Theorem; let us consider a Condorcetian reading of Hayek. Precisely because many people are making purchasing decisions, their aggregate judgments are highly likely to be correct, at least if most purchasers have relevant information. And simply because purchasers are purchasers, and hence are willing to put money on the line, they probably do have some such information, at least most of the time. Thus, Hayek's arguments can be seen to have a Condorcetian feature, but with a special twist: When people are willing to put their money where their mouth is, there is an increased likelihood that they will be right.

Why do prediction markets work? That, in a nutshell, is the answer.

/ Traditions: Burke as Hayekian, Hayek as Burkean? /

In fact, there is a connection between Hayek's claims and the views of Edmund Burke on the value of traditions and on the foolishness of trying to uproot them. In Burke's view, long-standing traditions, based on the judgments of many people over time, are far more reliable than decisions rooted in the judgments of particular people using the limited reason that each of them has. This is a bit of a detour, but it is worth pausing over the Burke-Hayek link here, because my focus thus far has been on aggregating knowledge across *space*. Burke's distinctive contribution is to show that knowledge is often aggregated across *time*; generalizing his work on prices and markets, Hayek saw the point as well.

In his most vivid passage, Burke writes:

> We wished at the period of the [English] Revolution, and do now wish, to derive all we possess as *an inheritance from our forefathers.* . . . The science of government being therefore so practical in itself, and intended for such practical purposes, a matter which requires experience, and even more experience than any person can gain in his whole life, however sagacious and observing he may be, it is with infinite caution than any man ought to venture upon pulling down an edifice which has answered in any tolerable degree, for ages the common purposes of society, or on building it up again, without having models and patterns of approved utility before his eyes. . . . *We are afraid to put men to live and trade each on his own private stock of reason; because we suspect that this stock in each man is small, and that the individuals would do better to avail themselves of the general bank and capital of nations, and of ages.* Many of our men of speculation, instead of

exploding general prejudices, employ their sagacity to discover the latent wisdom which prevails in them.[42]

Burke's most important claim opposes the small size of each "private stock of reason" to the "general bank and capital of nations, and of ages." In celebrating traditions, Burke's emphasis is on the need to resort to many minds, extending over time. In fact, the general idea of traditionalism, embodied in prominent forms of conservative political thought, can be best appreciated in this way. On one view, no reformer, or "expert," is likely to be in a good position to evaluate our practices, at least when the reformer or expert is compared with the countless people who have contributed to the creation and maintenance of those practices.

Hayek sees markets in much the same way that Burke saw traditions. Of course, Burke is able to invoke the test of time; if a practice lasts, then it is likely to have value and to make sense. But markets have an analogous test. If a product fails to work, or if it is wildly overpriced, it will fail the market's own test. Its price will fall or it will not continue to sell. Hayek himself made good use of Burke, seeing Burke as helping to form the intellectual tradition of which he considered himself a part, and suggesting that the utilitarian Jeremy Bentham, with his great faith in the reason of theorists, is in the opposite camp.[43]

In a fascinating essay on morality, Hayek built directly on his claims about prices to make explicitly Burkean claims (without, in this case, mentioning Burke). The core of Hayek's argument is that human morality is itself the product of many minds, making their decisions over long periods of time, in a way that produces a set of principles that no individual mind, and no theory, is likely to be able to capture. In his words, "Our morals endow us with capacities greater than our reason could do." Thus, his main claim is that "traditional morals may in some respects provide a surer guide to human action than rational knowledge," in areas ranging from respect for property to the family itself. In his most Burkean sentence, Hayek writes, "It is the humble recognition of the limitations of human reason which forces us to concede superiority to a moral order to which we owe our existence and which has its source *neither* in our innate instincts, which are still those of the savage, nor in our intelligence, which is not great enough to build better than it knows, but to a tradition which we must revere and care for even if we continuously experiment with improving its parts—not designing but humbly tinkering on a system which we must accept as given."[44] Hayek's claim, in short, is that many minds, extending over time, are responsible for morality itself.

Hayek may well have been wrong in seeing morality and culture as analogous to prices. The moral principles governing lying, or sex, or the family, or discrimination against women vary widely across groups and nations. It would be odd to say that any particular set of principles, at any moment in time, is a "price." Perhaps there is a kind of market for morality, extending over time. But even if this is so, it is not at all clear that moral principles *ought* simply to aggregate diverse views or dispersed knowledge. Consider, for example, the persistence of slavery and sex discrimination and the failure of traditional morality to do nearly as much as it might to help those with physical or mental disabilities.

For morality, a particular problem is that social pressures often force people to silence themselves, leaving hidden profiles. Many of us believe that morality requires some change from existing practice, but we do not want to incur the disapproval of other people. Recent illustrations include widespread but hidden support for the repeal of alcohol prohibition and for legalization of marijuana.[45] People are reluctant to express their views publicly on these topics, and they often engage in self-silencing on other moral issues, too.

What Hayek and Burke appear to miss is that traditional practices are often the congealed product of earlier informational or reputational cascades. Often morality consists of inefficient or unjust practices defended by entrenched groups and factions. A moral commitment, saying, for example, what people ought not to eat, might have made good sense in an earlier era, when the prohibited food carried disease. But in the modern period, the prohibition may make no sense. In an early time of human history, well-assigned sex roles, confining women to certain spheres, might have had some social justification (though perhaps not from the point of view of most women). But rigid sex roles lack solid or decent justifications today.

In many cases, traditions last not because they are excellent, but because influential people are averse to change and because of the sheer burdens of transition to a better state. It is for this reason that celebrations of traditions have always met an ambivalent reaction in free countries. Consider the exuberant words of James Madison, writing in a very young America:

But why is the experiment of an extended republic to be rejected, merely because it may comprise what is new? Is it not the glory of the people of America, that, whilst they have paid a decent regard to the opinions of former times and other nations, they have not suffered a blind veneration for antiquity, for custom, or for names, to overrule the suggestions of their own good sense, the knowledge of their own situation, and the lessons of their own experience? . . . Had no important step been taken by the leaders of the Revolution for which a precedent could not be discovered, no government established of which an exact model did not present itself, the people of the United States might, at this moment have been numbered among the melancholy victims of misguided councils, must at best have been laboring under the weight of some of those forms which have crushed the liberties of the rest of mankind. Happily for America, happily, we trust, for the whole human race, they pursued a new and more noble course. They accomplished a revolution which has no parallel in the annals of human society. They reared the fabrics of governments which have no model on the face of the globe.[46]

This is Madison's challenge to traditionalism. But the centerpiece of Hayek's argument involves markets and prices, and that is where its enduring value can be found.

/ Markets, Right and Wrong /

Hayek spoke of the price system in general, and it is natural to think that he was referring to ordinary commodities. But stock markets themselves have the properties that Hayek celebrates. Indeed, an influential theory of stock prices suggests that at any given time, such prices are "efficient" in the sense that they incorporate the information held by numerous traders, and are in that sense highly likely to be right.[47] On this view, it is not possible for individual traders to "beat the market." Because the market's prices are based on the judgments of many minds, its valuations are accurate, or at least more accurate than individual people are likely to be. Even the best experts lack the information that markets incorporate.

Of course, this optimistic view, known as the efficient capital markets hypothesis, has been subject to intense criticism, in part on the ground that stock prices are subject to many of the influences traced earlier in connection with deliberation.[48] I will engage and underline some of that criticism shortly. Let us begin with two obvious questions: What does it mean to be "right" about an ordinary commodity or a stock? Might Hayek have been too optimistic about the ability of markets to incorporate dispersed information? To understand the price system, and the uses of prediction markets, it is important to try to make some progress on these questions.

Everyone should agree that people are buying the wrong commodities if they could easily get better ones for less. If you pay $400 for a stereo when a better one is available next door for $200, you've blundered. If you buy lousy sneakers for $80 when you could easily find good ones for $40, there's a problem. Hayek's claims would be in trouble if it turned out that people are systematically paying high prices for bad products and low prices for good ones. A difficulty here is the immense variability of tastes. Products vary on many dimensions, and what you find to be a worse product might seem wonderful to others. Maybe the $80 sneakers look better, or even give special status to those who wear them. Because people care about their status, they might be willing to pay extra for products that do well on that count, even if they are otherwise merely serviceable.

The least ambitious reading of Hayek's argument is that because of market forces, and the incorporation of many minds, better products will have higher prices than worse ones, other things being equal. This claim seems obviously right as a general rule, but it's not all that exciting, and in any case, it isn't easy to test empirically.[49] A far more ambitious reading, consistent with neoclassical economics under certain assumptions, is that when free markets exist, prices will come to equal marginal cost. It is an empirical question whether this happens, and in many contexts it does not.

Why not? The simplest reason is that consumers have limited information and markets are not entirely free. Often consumers lack the knowledge that would permit them to do adequate comparison shopping. Sometimes government itself reduces the level of competition. Hence we should agree that the price system has significant advantages in its ability to incorporate information and to adjust to changes, without being at all clear whether prices, at any particular moment, can be said to be "right." For the reasons I have outlined, the price system will probably do better in setting prices than deliberating groups, which often prove unable to adjust with the provision of new information. But it is easy to think of cases in which products benefit from some kind of fad or fashion, ensuring wildly inflated prices by any objective measure. Informational cascades are common in the marketplace for such diverse goods as sneakers, movies, books, and gloves. Reputational cascades are pervasive as well. Often people buy goods not because they like them, but because they think that other people like them. The simple point is that the problems that infect deliberation play a significant role in markets, too.

For stock prices, the picture is even cloudier. The goal of investors is to make money. If the prices of some stocks are extremely low and about to rise, leaving neglected investment opportunities, then many minds aren't doing so well.

So, too, if the prices of some stocks are extremely high and about to fall, ensuring that many minds are losing a lot of money. Is it possible for stocks to be significantly overvalued or undervalued? Many specialists think so. Robert Shiller argues that the increase in the stock market from 1994 to 2000 was not justified "in any reasonable terms. Basic economic indicators did not come close to tripling," even though stock prices did. In that period, the ratio between stock prices and stock earnings was extreme by historical standards, with prices wildly inflated as compared to an objective measure of the profit-making ability of corporations.[50]

On this view, many minds were prone to error, leading to overvaluation. Shiller himself explains the inflation in prices by reference to psychological and social factors closely akin to those that infect deliberation. In particular, he argues that informational cascades and herd behavior very much affect stock prices, with investors following one another in a process of the blind leading the blind. In a fundamental challenge to Hayek's optimism about market processes, Shiller contends that the "same forces of human psychology that have driven the stock market over the years have the potential to affect other markets."[51]

/ Prediction Markets, Right and Wrong /

The debate over valuation of stocks and real estate remains a vigorous one. It is clear that individual investors make a lot of mistakes. But some people continue to believe that Hayek's general analysis remains valid and that, all things considered, prices are extremely accurate over time, or at least more accurate than any alternative. Let us put these complex debates to one side. The beauty of prediction markets is that they allow a simple test for accuracy: Did the market price accurately predict the future? As we have seen, the answer is often yes. In addition to the examples given thus far, consider the fact that of the many diverse predictions on Strategymarkets.com, the market has been right well over 90 percent of the time.

At first glance, Hayek's arguments about the price system offer a simple explanation of why prediction markets work: Information is widely dispersed in society, and prediction markets take advantage of that dispersed information. But it should be immediately apparent that there is a major difference between the price system and prediction markets. As Hayek emphasized, individual people know, above all, about their own tastes. They know what they like; if food doesn't taste so good, if shoes are uncomfortable, or if a newly designed car is ugly, people will respond. In sharp contrast, prediction markets do not take advantage of people's unique access to their own tastes, and in this way they lack a key feature of ordinary markets. But even the market for investments does not involve tastes of this sort: When people invest in stocks, bonds, or real estate, they are hoping, not to indulge their tastes, but to make money. Whether they make money will depend on a prediction. And if ordinary investment markets work well, then prediction markets should work well, too.

One reason for the current success rate is that accurate answers can emerge even if only a small percentage of participants have good information. This is a crucial point. Deliberating groups often operate on a principle of "one person, one vote"; but in a prediction market, intense preferences, based on really good information, can be counted as such. In the Iowa Electronic Markets, for example, it turns out that 85 percent of the traders do not seem to be particularly wise.[52] They hold on to their shares for a long period and then simply accept someone else's prices. The predictions of the market are largely driven by the other 15 percent: frequent traders who post their offers rather than accepting those made by other people.

To work well, prediction markets do not require accurate judgments by anything like the majority of participants. In this sense, prediction markets are very different from the ordinary judgments of deliberating groups. The resulting prices do not amplify or perpetuate cognitive errors. On the contrary, they correct them, because shrewd traders are able to invest in a way that fixes even widespread errors.

Of course, prediction markets involve a measure of deliberation. Many individual investors deliberate with friends, family, and others before they invest. In some such markets, investors undoubtedly act in teams, pooling resources after deliberating together about what to do. The point is that ultimately conclusions come not from asking group members to come up with a mutually agreeable conclusion, but by reference to the price signal, which will have aggregated a great deal of diverse information. It is for this reason that prediction markets often outperform deliberative processes.

/ Building on Markets /

How might groups and institutions take advantage of prediction markets? It is possible to imagine both internal and external varieties. An internal market would be limited to people within the relevant organization. As we have seen, Hewlett Packard has used such a market to predict sales, Google has used a similar market to project its own development, and the Department of Defense proposed an internal Policy Analysis Market, limited to its own employees, as part of its abandoned initiative on geopolitical events. An external market would permit public investment by people outside of the institution for which predictions are being made.

An organization might rely on an internal market if it seeks to keep the results private or if it believes that an aggregation of information held within the organization will be sufficiently accurate. One risk of an internal market is that it might be too thin simply because most institutions will have few investors;[53] another is that members of the organization might suffer from a systematic bias. Aware of these risks, an institution might create a public market, available to all, believing that through this route it will obtain more accurate results. In either case, an organization might use a prediction market instead of group deliberation, or at the very least as an input into such deliberation. Consider a few possibilities:

1. Regulators are greatly interested in trends involving air pollution, including increases or decreases in emissions over time and also in concentrations of pollutants in the ambient air. A prediction market might make projections about sulfur dioxide and particulate concentrations in New York City, Chicago, and Los Angeles in the next year or decade.

2. It is important both for government and for outside observers to know the size of federal budget deficits. Government projections are greatly disputed, and some of them might well be self-serving. Prediction markets might provide more reliable estimates.[54]

3. Regulators might be concerned about the likely risks of a new disease, or of an old disease that seems to be growing in magnitude. To assess the risks, they might create a prediction market designed to project the

number of deaths that will be attributed to, for example, flu or mad cow disease over a specified period.

4. Federal and state agencies monitor a range of institutions to ensure that they are solvent.[55] One problem is that such agencies do not know whether insolvencies are likely to be many or few in a particular year; another is that the solvency of particular institutions can be difficult to predict in advance. Prediction markets could help with both problems.[56]

5. The national government might want to know the number of people who are likely to be infected by HIV in the United States or Africa by the year 2010; the answer to that question might be relevant to its policy judgments. A prediction market might be used to make forecasts about the future progress of the disease.[57] Such markets might generally be used to make forecasts about the likely effects of development projects, such as those involving vaccinations and mortality reductions.[58]

6. The Central Intelligence Agency might want to know about the outcome of elections in Iraq, or the likelihood of a feared event in the Middle East. The CIA might create an internal prediction market, designed to aggregate the information held by its own employees.

7. The White House might seek to predict the likelihood and magnitude of damage from natural disasters, including tornadoes and earthquakes. Accurate information could greatly assist in advance planning. Prediction markets could easily be created to help in that task.

Some of these examples involve private behavior. Others involve the judgments of public institutions. Some might seem fanciful. Others involve predictions on which prediction markets are already flourishing.

Failed Predictions? Of Manipulation, Bias, and Bubbles /

In what circumstances might prediction markets fail? Let's begin with some noteworthy blunders. In 2005, it was widely rumored that Chief Justice William Rehnquist would retire shortly after the end of the Supreme Court's term in June. An informational cascade quickly arose. People said that the chief justice would resign, not because they knew, but because other people said that the chief justice would resign. The cascade reached influential members of the media and even the U.S. Senate, leading them to join and hence to amplify the cascade. Prediction markets similarly foresaw his retirement. Nonetheless, he elected to stay on the bench until his death in September. Notwithstanding their confidence, notwithstanding the economic incentives, and notwithstanding Hayek, the investors were badly wrong.

Tradesports.com hosted a prediction market attempting to predict the identity of President George W. Bush's first nominee to the Supreme Court. Until roughly two hours before the official announcement, the market was more or less completely ignorant of the existence of John Roberts, the actual nominee. The official announcement took place on July 19, 2005. At the close of the market on July 18, "shares" in then-Judge Roberts were trading at $0.19, representing an estimate that he had a 1.9 percent chance of being nominated. Indeed, shares in Chief Justice Roberts did not rise higher than $5 until 6:34 p.m. Eastern Standard Time, a mere two and a half hours before the nomination. Chief Justice Roberts did not become the favorite until 7:40 p.m., about the same time that President Bush began contacting Senate leaders to inform them of his choice.

The Tradesports market also fell victim to an informational cascade, one that in retrospect seems almost comical.

Throughout the day of the Roberts announcement, it was widely rumored that President Bush would select Judge Edith Clement. These rumors represented a cascade in action. Many people were saying that the president would select Judge Clement, not because they knew, but because other people were saying that the president would select Judge Clement. Once new people joined the chorus, the pro-Clement music became very loud, so much so that it seemed foolish not to sing along. The market was exceedingly responsive to those rumors. Shares of Judge Clement peaked around $8 and remained high all morning. Shortly before 5 p.m., wire services began reporting that Judge Clement was not the nominee, a report that produced a precipitous drop within a few minutes. In short, the market reflected the conventional wisdom, and it was clueless about Judge Clement's prospects.

Is it possible to generalize from the failures of prediction markets with respect to the Rehnquist resignation and the Roberts nomination? An initial possibility: Maybe prediction markets know nothing about the U.S. Supreme Court! A more helpful and general point is that such markets work well only when there is a great deal of dispersed information to aggregate. Consider another unsuccessful prediction: Would weapons of mass destruction be found in Iraq? For some of 2003, the Tradesports.com market set the likelihood at over 80 percent; for much of the year, the likelihood was 50 percent or higher. Traders were reluctant to bet against the apparently strong arguments made by President Bush's White House, and the market lacked dispersed information that traders could use, or obtain, to produce a contrary prediction.[59]

Recall that the theoretical foundation for prediction markets can be found in Hayek's work on prices. Suppose that a company sells watches; suppose that these watches sometimes lose significant time over the course of a year or two. Eventually, people will learn that fact, and the dispersed information will affect the demand for the product. With stock markets, investors use dispersed information as well. But there is no such information about whether a Supreme Court justice will resign, and across a range of possible candidates, investors lack dispersed information about the president's likely choice. A worldwide prediction market is unlikely to do so well in foreseeing the first book I will read in the next calendar year, or what you are going to have for dinner tomorrow night.

Consider another unsuccessful prediction. In late 2005, there was a great deal of speculation about whether Patrick Fitzgerald, the special prosecutor, would indict Karl Rove, President Bush's chief of staff, for criminal conduct in connection with the disclosure of the name of a CIA agent. The results of the prediction market on Tradesports.com appear in Figure 4.2.

On October 27, the market predicted that Rove would be indicted, with a likelihood of 65 percent. On October 28, Fitzgerald indicted the vice president's chief of staff, Scooter Libby, and failed to indict Rove. Hence, the prediction shifted dramatically, to one of no indictment for Rove. Why did the earlier prediction fail? The obvious answer is that with respect to the ultimate decision of Patrick Fitzgerald, investors had little information to aggregate. They did have some information, of course, but this was not a situation like an Oscar winner, or an outcome of an election, where a great deal of publicly dispersed knowledge could be turned into an accurate "price."

This is the most fundamental limitation of prediction markets: They cannot work well unless investors have

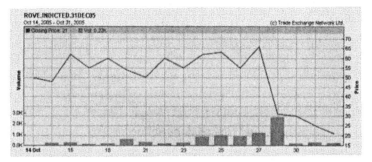

Figure 4.2

dispersed information that can be aggregated. But there are other potential problems, and to see them, ordinary stock markets are the place to start. As I have suggested, a great deal of recent attention has been paid to the possibility that individual traders are manipulable and also subject to identifiable biases.[60] There is also a risk of "bubbles," leading markets to make inaccurate judgments about stocks or future events. Hayek was right to say that the price system has major advantages over any central planner in incorporating dispersed information. But his account of prices was too optimistic, even starry-eyed. With effective marketing, products can sell quite well, even if they aren't so good. Stocks can be wildly overvalued, and overvaluation can persist for significant periods. For all their promise, prediction markets are subject to similar risks.

Manipulation /

A primary concern is that prediction markets, no less than ordinary ones, can be manipulated by powerful speculators.[61] An attempt to manipulate a prediction market occurred during the 2000 presidential election. A group of speculators tried to manipulate the IEM by buying large volumes of futures in presidential candidate Patrick Buchanan. The value of Buchanan shares did increase dramatically, but they fell almost immediately when well-informed traders profited at the expense of the manipulative traders.[62] The Iowa market remained stable despite this attempted manipulation. Perhaps other, more determined efforts at manipulation would succeed, but none has thus far.

Biases /

The results are unequivocal: Just as in group deliberation, investors in a market are subject to predictable heuristics and biases. For example, psychologists have found that people overestimate the likelihood that their own preferred candidate will win an election, a form of *optimistic bias*.[63] At a certain point in the 1980 campaign, 87 percent of Jimmy Carter's supporters believed that he would win, and 80 percent of Ronald Reagan's supporters believed that their candidate would win.[64] Obviously, at least one side greatly overestimated its candidate's probability of victory (Carter's, as it happened).

Is it shocking to hear that some gamblers in New York are particularly likely to bet on the New York Yankees?[65] IEM traders show the same bias. In 1988, Michael Dukakis supporters were more likely to hold futures in the Massachusetts governor's ill-fated presidential bid than were supporters of his opponent, George H. W. Bush.[66] More striking still, Dukakis supporters were more likely to view the candidates' debates as helpful to the Democratic candidate. After each debate. Dukakis supporters bought futures in the Massachusetts governor's ill-fated presidential bid, and supporters of his opponent, George H. W. Bush, bought Bush futures.[67]

Human beings usually assimilate new information in a way that confirms their view of the world; this phenomenon is called *confirmation bias*. Those who invest in prediction markets show that bias.[68] Undoubtedly, many investors lose money in the stock market for exactly the same reason. In general, traders show a tendency to buy and sell in a way that fits with their party identification.[69]

Despite all this, the IEM proved extremely accurate, even more so than polls, in predicting the outcome of the 1988 presidential election. No less than three weeks before the election, the market provided an almost perfect guess about the candidates' shares of the vote.[70] The simple finding is that, *although many people are biased, the markets as a whole are not.* How is such accuracy possible when many traders are prone to blunder?

The likely answer lies in the *marginal trader hypothesis*, which emphasizes the behavior of a small group of traders who are far less susceptible to biases. According to this hypothesis, certain traders, not showing the relevant biases, have a disproportionately large effect on prices. In election markets, these traders are able to earn significant profits at the expense of other traders.[71] If marginal traders are active and able to profit from the errors and biases of other participants, then errors and biases will have no effect on the aggregate market price—a real testimony to Hayek.

A distinct bias that might be expected to affect prediction markets is the *favorite–long shot bias*, often seen in horse races. In horse racing, heavy favorites tend to produce higher returns than other horses in the field, whereas long shots tend to offer lower-than-expected returns.[72] The same bias is seen in tennis matches, where the best players get higher returns and the lower-ranked players attract a disproportionate share of bets.[73] In these domains, bettors undervalue near certainties and overvalue low probabilities. If this point holds in general,[74] prediction markets might not be accurate with respect to highly improbable events. The market should be expected to overestimate the likelihood that such events will come to fruition. But with respect to existing prediction markets, there is at best modest evidence of systematic errors in this vein.[75]

In some markets, of course, biased traders do mean biased markets. As we have seen, the stock market of the late 1990s is an example, and the whole field of behavioral finance attempts to explain how biased markets can persist over time.[76] But prediction markets have generally been free from this problem. We will undoubtedly be learning a great deal about this topic.

Bubbles and More /

I have noted that the stock market contains bubbles, in which stocks trade well above their fundamental value. Bubbles often occur when people believe, not that a stock is really worth a great deal, but that other people *think* that the stock is worth a great deal. People invest with the expectation that value will increase because of the enthusiasm of other people.[77]

Can bubbles occur on prediction markets? Of course they can. "Prediction bubbles" are easy to imagine, with investors moving in a certain direction with the belief that many other investors are doing the same. A temporary upsurge in investment in Hillary Rodham Clinton as the 2004 Democratic nominee might well have been a small bubble, with some investors thinking, not that she would in fact be the nominee, but that others would invest in that judgment, thus inflating the value of the investment. And if bubbles are possible, crashes are possible, too.

In any case, informational influences certainly can lead people to make foolish investments in any market, including those involving predictions. Informational cascades play a role in investment decisions, just as in choices about what products to buy. A fad might suddenly benefit a sneaker company, a book, a television program, a restaurant, a movie, a stock, or an investment opportunity of any kind. Many people might be attracted to one of these, not because they have independent information that the product is good, or even because they believe that it is much better than the alternatives, but simply because they are following the signals provided by the cascade. So, too, for "hot" predictions; recall the cascades in favor of the retirement of Chief Justice William Rehnquist and rumored Supreme Court nominee Judge Edith Clement.

Hayek did not much grapple with the risk that markets will suffer from herd behavior. If he had, his best response would be that smart investors will be alert to that risk and more than willing to take advantage of it. If herds of people ensure that a product or a stock is a bargain, then other people—first a few, then a lot—will purchase it, and the market will eventually correct itself.

But experience shows that this view can be too optimistic, at least for ordinary stocks.[78] As prediction markets develop, significant individual errors should be expected, and undoubtedly they will produce some errors in the price signal. Consider the 2004 presidential election. On the day of the vote, dramatic news of pro-Kerry exit polls produced not only a huge switch in the conventional wisdom in the media and on blogs, but also a great deal of volatility in election markets, with a wild swing in the direction of Senator Kerry at the expense of President Bush. "Suddenly, Kerry's stock in the Winner Take All market shot up to 70 cents and Bush stock was in the cellar."[79] The rumors affected investors, not just onlookers.

Large-scale errors are always possible when apparently relevant news leads numerous investors to buy or sell. Indeed, election day in 2004 may well have been a cascade, with investors responding to one another's judgments, even though they were based on misleading information. But for those enthusiastic about prediction markets, there is some favorable evidence: The erroneous figures were able to last for only a few hours, after which the numbers returned to their previous state of accuracy.

In some contexts, the imaginable problems go well beyond the risk of bubbles. Consider the problem of terrorism futures. Of course, any nation would benefit if it could aggregate privately held information about the risk and likely location of a terrorist attack. But do investors actually possess helpful information? When betting on presidential elections, people can use ordinary information sources, along with their network of friends, family, and coworkers, to form an opinion. For the vast majority of investors, there are no such sources of information about terrorist activity. Perhaps terrorist futures would fail for the same reason that prediction markets cannot foresee the president's Supreme Court nominations: Sufficiently dispersed information is unavailable.

In any event, government use of the resulting information could be self-defeating, at least if the information were made public. Terrorists would know the anticipated time and location of attacks and also know that the government was aware of these, which would make it most unlikely that the prediction would turn out to be accurate. Where the event's occurrence is likely to be affected by the outcome of the information market, there is reason for skepticism about the market's likely performance.[80]

But many policy issues, including those potentially involved in the now-defunct Policy Analysis Market, do not have this feature. Consider, for example, the question whether the Egyptian economy is likely to grow in the next year, or whether a Palestinian state will be created by a specified date. Maybe many investors will lack a great deal of information on such questions, but it is most unlikely that the market prediction will turn out to be self-defeating. Of course, any Policy Analysis Market itself raises many questions. The only point is that in many domains, prediction markets have worked extremely well, and they are likely to outperform both statistical means and the products of group deliberation.

/ Feasible Futures /

Prediction markets face a pervasive problem of feasibility. Suppose that Congress is deciding whether to authorize stem cell research. That decision calls for judgments of value, not merely of fact, and no information market can make judgments of value. How could a political leader submit questions about abortion, capital punishment, and preemptive war to a prediction market? For many of the most important questions that societies face, prediction markets will not be adequate, even if they incorporate the views of many minds and hence produce a ton of information.

To be sure, such markets might be used to predict what juries will do; as we have seen, prediction markets successfully predicted the acquittal of singer Michael Jackson. (Here's a prediction: In the future, prediction markets will mostly make accurate predictions about jury decisions.) But a jury could not use such markets to decide on questions of guilt or innocence. There is no objective way to test whether the jury ended up with the right answer. (If there were, the jury would be dispensable!) Nor is it easy to see how prediction markets could be used by judges. Of course, factual questions are often relevant in court, but such markets could not easily be used to verify one or another answer.

There is another problem. When the relevant groups are small, effective markets may be impossible to create simply because there are not enough investors.[81] A certain number is necessary to ensure that markets have enough information to aggregate. On the other hand, ambitious efforts are under way to examine how government might use prediction markets to answer an array of disputed questions. At a minimum, such markets should be used, where feasible, as an adjunct to deliberative processes.

Prediction markets remain in their early stages. We have seen that in many domains, they perform extremely well— better than surveys, better than deliberating groups, better than experts. Their promise is most likely to be realized when knowledge is genuinely dispersed, when a wide range of people know relevant facts, and when their incentives lead them to reveal, through investments, what they know.

Consider the famous bet between Julian Simon and Paul Ehrlich about the likely scarcity of natural resources.[82] Simon had long predicted that natural resources were essentially inexhaustible, whereas Ehrlich believed that natural resources were running out. In 1980, the two bet on the price of five metals to be selected by Ehrlich: If, by 1990, the price of the metals had risen (suggesting scarcity), Ehrlich would win. Ehrlich chose copper, chrome, nickel, tin, and tungsten. He lost the bet. By 1990, the price of each of the five metals had fallen. I am willing to predict that prediction markets would have strongly sided with Simon. (I'd be happy to bet on that.)

The simple upshot is that in many cases, private or public institutions might create markets to provide information on important questions, and public institutions might take that information into account in deciding what to do. In Hayek's spirit, the best way to start is with the prediction markets run by the private sector, which has made productive use of such markets in the past and which promises to do much more of the same in the future. Prediction markets need not be a substitute for deliberation. But if deliberators choose to ignore what they say, they ought to have a good reason for doing so.

Chapter Five / **Many Working Minds: Wikis, Open Source Software, and Blogs**

Prediction markets are a simple way to aggregate private information, and the Internet has greatly contributed to their growth. But with the Internet, countless other methods are available. Every day, companies are taking advantage of information from many minds to see what particular minds will find appealing. Consider *collaborative filtering*, the process of figuring out what you're likely to like by investigating the tastes of minds that are like yours. Amazon.com is a familiar example: A computer program identifies the preferences of those who have bought what you bought, and it generates a series of recommendations that are likely to match your tastes. The recommendations can be eerily good.

Netflix.com is more elaborate. You are asked to rate the movies you see. On the basis of those ratings, Netflix identifies your tastes, and then matches them with people with similar tastes. Through this process, Netflix is able to predict how you'll like movies that you haven't yet seen. Many people report that the predictions are uncannily accurate.

I have referred to the idea of the Daily Me, a personal newspaper that caters to your particular tastes. With the Daily Me, you can filter out everything that you don't like and filter in whatever best fits your tastes. As it turns out, we don't need to create a Daily Me. It can be created for us, precisely because producers have access to many minds, some of which are eerily close to ours. No one may be a perfect match for you—perhaps your enthusiasm for Sheryl Crow fits poorly with your other tastes—but collaborative filtering works exceptionally well. It can even build cocoons.

The question for that process, however, is relatively narrow; it is how to discern the tastes of one person by learning the tastes of others. My question here is much broader: What mechanisms can be used to elicit the dispersed knowledge held by many minds, allowing them to contribute to products and activities that concern us?

Let us focus on three possibilities: wikis, open source software, and blogs. The three have important commonalities and also noteworthy differences. They offer distinct models for how groups, large or small, might gather information and interact on the Internet. They provide important supplements to, or substitutes for, ordinary deliberation. They might even be seen as central places in which deliberation is now occurring—with increasing social importance.

Of course, wikis, open source software, and blogs are only three mechanisms for aggregating information; new ones will inevitably emerge. My hope is that an understanding of these methods will be helpful not only for its own sake, but also as a means of appreciating initiatives that are now just beginning, or that remain mere fantasy. In the domain of information aggregation, things are changing with amazing speed, but we know enough to have a sense of what is on the horizon.

/ Wikis, Wikipedia, Flu Wiki, and Beyond /

Wiki World /

A wiki is a Web site that allows any user to add material and to edit and delete what previous users have done. The term comes from the Hawaiian word *wikiwiki*, which means "fast" or "speedy." (That term may well come from the

English word "quick"; if "quick" were translated into Hawaiian phonology, *wiki* or *kiwiki* would be the result.) The concept of the wiki originated with Ward Cunningham, who sought to produce "the simplest online database that could possibly work."[1] In 1994, Cunningham developed the initial wiki server, which provided an exceptionally easy means of editing and which invited contributions from anyone who wanted to edit or add material.[2]

In the enthusiastic words of Cunningham and his coauthor Bol Leuf, "Wiki is *inherently democratic*—every user has exactly the same capabilities as any other user."[3] Cunningham's own wiki is thoroughly democratic in that sense. Other wiki software, such as the widely used MediaWiki, includes special support for "administrators" with greater powers than other users. Nonetheless, wikis are democratic in the sense that they permit anyone to edit pages.

At first glance, the democratic quality of wikis seems to be a big problem. If anyone in the world can make changes, isn't the text vulnerable to pranks and even destruction? Isn't some kind of security needed to protect against malevolent people? Cunningham and Leuf say that "experience shows that in fact little damage is done to wiki content even in the absence of security mechanisms."[4] If this is so, it is not because of economic incentives, as in prediction markets. It is because most people really want the process to work. An important current use of wikis is to create documentation for technical projects, and many free and open source software projects now use wiki as the preferred format for creating such documentation.

Wikipedia /

Of course, software projects are not everyone's cup of tea. To date, the most notable wiki, by far, is Wikipedia, a free,

Web-based encyclopedia that attempts to take advantage of the information held by its tens of thousands of contributors ("Wikipedians"), who add to and edit the encyclopedia. (Try it, if you like; it's easy.) Wikipedia is written and edited by these numerous volunteers, who can change and add articles however they wish. Its remarkable goal is nothing less than "to distribute a free encyclopedia to every single person on the planet in their own language."[5]

Wikipedia is growing at an explosive rate, and any numbers will rapidly become obsolete. At the present time, there are more than 2 million articles, approaching 1 million in English (amounting to more than 200 million words) and the rest in about two hundred other languages, of which only about half are active. (There is a Wikipedia in Klingon, the fictional language of a race of violence-prone but basically honorable humanoids created on the television show *Star Trek*.) There are nine "major" Wikipedias, with more than fifty thousand articles; twenty-one minor Wikipedias, with more than ten thousand articles; the rest are less active. Interestingly, the growth of the Arabic Wikipedia has been slowed by virtue of the fact that most Arabic Internet users speak English well, and they have been writing Wikipedia entries for the English Wikipedia.

Tens of millions of people visit Wikipedia every day, making it one of the world's most popular sites, more popular than the *New York Times* and even PayPal. The number of visitors, like the number of articles, is rapidly growing. The range is astonishing. If a person suddenly achieves public importance—through election, appointment, or sheer celebrity—it is almost certain that Wikipedia will have a relevant article almost immediately. The article is often detailed; it is nearly always highly informative.

Wikipedia grows out of an old-fashioned, less imaginative, and now-abandoned project, Nupedia, an early effort to create a free encyclopedia on the Internet. Nupedia was structured like an ordinary encyclopedia, with expert writers and a system of peer review. Unfortunately, if also unsurprisingly, the process of writing Nupedia proved exceptionally slow. As a result, Jimmy "Jimbo" Wales, the founder of Nupedia, was persuaded to supplement it with a more informal project, in which ordinary people could write and edit entries. Started on January 10, 2001, Wikipedia had one thousand articles by February, ten thousand by September 7, and forty thousand by August 30, 2002. As early as May 2001, Wikipedias were created in many other languages, including Catalan, Chinese, Dutch, German, Esperanto, French, Hebrew, Italian, Portuguese, Spanish, and Swedish.

It is an understatement to say that Wikipedia generally works. In terms of sheer volume, it dwarfs the *Encyclopedia Britannica*. The number of articles is extraordinary. True, the quality does not always match the quantity; you can easily find articles that are thin or amateurish or that contain significant omissions and errors. But for the most part, the quality tends to be high as well. Specialists are regularly surprised to see a great deal of accuracy, as well as astounding currency, in Wikipedia entries; the millions of visitors are responding to the fact that they have a lot to learn. In a way, this is a real mystery. Why is Wikipedia so successful?

An essential part of the answer is that large numbers of knowledgeable people are willing to participate in creating Wikipedia, and whatever errors they make usually receive rapid correction, simply because so many minds are involved. The involvement of many people ensures that Wikipedians are able to produce a much more comprehensive resource than a small group could, even a small group of experts. Amazing but true: Wikipedia is revised hundreds of times every hour. At last count, more than seven hundred articles were being added every *day*. Wikipedia is thus able to elicit widely dispersed information. But the large set of contributors disguises some distinctive features of this particular wiki. For the English edition, over half of the edits are done by 0.7 percent of all users—a mere 524 people. The most active 2 percent of users, that is, fewer than fifteen hundred people, have done almost three-quarters of all edits. For the Spanish Wikipedia, 8.1 percent of all users produce more than 90 percent of edits. Wikipedia thus combines huge numbers of occasional volunteers with a not-so-huge core of frequent editors.

Wikipedia is in part a deliberative forum, with reason-giving by those who disagree and with deliberative "places" to accompany disagreement. In fact, every page on MediaWiki, used by Wikipedia, includes an accompanying "talk" page. This means that every entry in the encyclopedia can be used as a deliberative space—and many entries are so used.

Wikipedia also has the huge advantage of cumulative knowledge. An initial entry might be thin. In fact, thin entries are described as "stubs," inviting more sustained treatment. In Wikipedia's own words, "Stubs are articles which have not yet received substantial attention from the Wikipedia editors. They have been created, but don't yet contain enough information to be truthfully considered articles. The community believes that stubs are far from worthless. They are, rather, the first step articles take on their course to becoming complete." Over a short period of time, stubs and thin entries do become much thicker.

It is even possible to think of Wikipedia as an exceptionally fast-moving tradition: Everyone who edits is standing on the shoulders of those who were there earlier. It isn't easy to write an entry from scratch, especially on a technical topic. But if thousands of people are in a position to make small additions and improvements, an initial skeleton can rapidly become a full body. In the anyone-can-edit words of the site itself, "We are working together on statements of what is known (what constitutes free human knowledge) about various subjects. Each of us individually benefits from this arrangement. It is difficult to single-handedly write *the perfect article*, but it becomes easier when working to-gether. . . . We *assume that the world is full of reasonable people* and that collectively they can arrive eventually at a reasonable conclusion, despite the worst efforts of a very few wreckers."[6] Quality control occurs through a kind of peer review, in which new edits appear on a "recent changes" page that is often examined by many people each day.

This attitude leads to a distinctive and, in a way, remark-able attitude toward authorship. On Wikipedia, no person considers himself "the" author of an entry. With wikis in general, the concept of authorship is discouraged and, in a way, senseless; it is disconnected from the very notion of a wiki. Many people consider it "unwiki" to proclaim author-ship, or principal authorship, of an entry. Blogs, which I take up shortly, are very different on this count. To be sure, many bloggers release their content under a special kind of license, known as a Creative Commons License, which generally allows free distribution of copyrighted works so long as credit is given. (The development of the Creative Commons License, launched by Lawrence Lessig, is worth emphasizing; because copying is permitted without causing copyright problems, this license promotes access to material by many minds. Wikipedia uses the GNU Free Documentation License, which also rejects standard copyright restrictions in favor of much freer use.) But bloggers usually protect their authorship by asking that they be credited for ideas and texts. Wikipedia works even though authorship is not rewarded or even claimed.

Of course, there are risks of error, partiality, and vandalism on wikis. People may believe that something is true about evolution, or George W. Bush, or Fidel Castro, or life on other planets, or the Catholic Church, but the belief may be mistaken. Wikipedia works because those who know the truth, or something close to it, are usually more numerous and more committed than those who believe in a falsehood. The site explains, again in prose that anyone can edit, "In all honesty, Wikipedia has a fair bit of well-meaning, but ill-informed and amateurish work. In fact, we welcome it—an amateurish article to be improved later is better than nothing. In any case, when new hands (particularly, experts on the subjects in question) arrive and go to work, the amateurish work is usually straightened out. Really egregious errors are fixed quickly by the thousands of people who read Wikipedia every day. In general, the worse the error, the faster it will be noticed and fixed."

This may be an excessively sunny view of the situation. Some of the entries aren't very good. In areas that involve technology, Wikipedia tends to shine, often outperforming ordinary encyclopedias—a tribute to the technology-savvy participants that it attracts. But in my own field of law, the quality is more mixed, especially in complex areas. Even in law, however, most of the entries are at least serviceable, and it is true that those that are really bad tend to be corrected, often promptly, especially when and because certain pages are watched by editors and authors.

There is a deeper issue. In some areas, what is true is greatly disputed, and it is hard to find an impartial arbiter. If anyone in the world can serve as an editor, partisans should be able to move content in their preferred directions, making entries quite unreliable. We could easily imagine a situation in which liberals or conservatives skew relevant articles, hoping to influence opinions and perhaps even the outcome of elections. In response to this risk, Wikipedia maintains a general policy of neutrality, and in the event that the policy seems to be violated, Wikipedia offers an ingenious solution: a red "Stop Hand," supplemented by the simple statement, "The neutrality of this article is disputed."[7] In fact, there is a (very) long list of articles whose neutrality is disputed.[8] A recent list, with more than twelve hundred entries, included articles on Jimmy Carter, monogamy, libertarianism, lawyer, Noam Chomsky, Nation of Islam, Palestinian National Authority, Richard Nixon, persecution of Christians, rape, sexism, terrorism, Vietnam War, Fidel Castro, sport utility vehicle, AIDS conspiracy theories, and New Jersey(!). The large number of disputed articles is causing some consternation in the Wikipedia community.

When active debates are occurring about the content of articles, it is necessary to have good norms to provide some discipline. The term "Wikiquette" refers to the etiquette that Wikipedians follow. Wikiquette helps to ensure that the active debates are transferred to separate "talk pages." These are the deliberative forums on Wikipedia, in which those who disagree explain the basis for their disagreement. What is noteworthy is that the articles themselves are (mostly) solid, and that partisan debates have a specifically designed location. Sometimes those debates end up producing shared judgments that can, in turn, be found in articles.

To be sure, vandalism is a potentially serious problem. As Wikipedia is constructed, only an administrator can permanently delete pages. But anyone in the world can make a temporary change or deletion, which will show up on any computer in the world with Internet access. Spamming is also possible. People might alter an entry to make it a string of obscenities, or to turn it into nonsense, or to insert deliberate errors, or simply to cause chaos. In 2005, one vandal wrote that John Seigenthaler Sr., a prominent journalist, may have been involved in the assassination of both President John F. Kennedy and his brother Robert Kennedy; this erroneous statement stayed on Wikipedia for four months before it was taken down. Another vandal has repeatedly added images of Darth Vader to various pages; yet another added fake death notices to the pages of prominent Democratic politicians; other vandals have created nonsense pages. But in general, Wikipedia has done exceedingly well in combating these problems. It describes its own practice as "something along the lines of vigilante justice." This means that individual readers can "revert" the page to the most recent good version or mark the page as one that ought to be deleted.

Readers are also permitted to identify persistent vandals and to suggest that they be added to the "vandalism in progress" page. Such vandals can eventually be blocked by Wikipedia's technology (allowing IP blocking or username blocking). Wikipedia works because the vandals are hopelessly outnumbered by those who want to make the project work.

Why Wikis Work (or Not) /
It is tempting and helpful to explain the success of Wikipedia through Hayek's distinctive lens. Jimmy Wales himself has drawn the connection, saying, "Hayek's work on price theory is central to my own thinking about how to manage the Wikipedia project. Possibly one can understand Wikipedia

without understanding Hayek. . . . But one can't understand my ideas about Wikipedia without understanding Hayek."[9] Certainly, Wikipedia entries often aggregate the information held by numerous people in a way that connects closely to Hayek's claims about the price system. If information is widely dispersed, and if no single "planner" has access to what is known, then Wikipedia's method of operations has the same general justification as the price system. As central planners relate to markets, so, in a way, do standard encyclopedias relate to Wikipedia.

Indeed, we can go much further. Perhaps any particular article, at any particular time, should be seen as a kind of "price" that is a product of many minds and that might be altered, at least to some extent, by any interested person. As we have seen, a price is a result of the judgments and tastes of a large number of consumers. An article on Wikipedia or any other wiki has the same characteristic.

But this is only a metaphor. Wikipedia does not involve or set prices, and here there is an initial and major difference between wikis on the one hand and the price system on the other. In addition, most Wikipedians do not stand to gain or lose by adding information. There are no trades and no mutually advantageous deals. The economic incentive that underlies market behavior usually plays no role in Wikipedia. For many users, participation is attributable not to self-interest, but to other motivations, including people's desire to see their words in print, the value of self-expression, and the apparently widespread desire to be helpful and constructive. To the extent that the economic incentive is generally more reliable than these motivations, Wikipedia's success may not be so easy to replicate. But for many wikis, money and self-interest are apparently less important than economists, at least, tend to think.

A qualification: It is possible to become an enfranchised voter in major decisions about Wikipedia's future (consider the question whether Wikimedia should create a new service of one or another kind). Those who make enough edits to be considered active users obtain the franchise. Some Wikipedians make large numbers of small edits (involving grammar and spelling) to obtain this more powerful status. In this sense, status and reputation can play a significant role in wiki communities, a point to which I return in the context of open source software.

There is another difference between the price system and wikis. In wikis, the last editor can be a self-appointed dictator; in the price system, individual consumers almost never have any such role. If you really like chocolate ice cream, you will probably buy a lot of chocolate ice cream, but your purchases will not much affect the price. But on Wikipedia, you can delete an entry or enter false information, at least until you are caught. If you are confused and add errors, those errors can dominate the story, whatever your predecessors said. I have emphasized that Wikipedia has safeguards against vandalism and that Wikipedians are good at correcting errors. But the last editor has an authority far greater than that of the last purchaser or seller of a product.

For this reason, it should be easy to see that Wikipedia need not always incorporate the multiple diverse views of its editors. Because the last editor can appoint himself as sovereign, no aggregation may occur at all (even though editors who behave inappropriately end up with a brief reign). In the price system, an individual consumer cannot easily become a self-appointed sovereign. President John F. Kennedy's father is said to have purchased forty thousand copies of his son's book, *Profiles in Courage*, to put that book on the best-seller list; but such behavior is rare in markets. Because Wikipedia uses a "last in time" rule, because no literal price is created, and because economic incentives are not directly involved, Hayek's central arguments about that "marvel," the price system, do not apply, at least not directly.

In this light, we can easily imagine a society in which Wikipedia would not work. Imagine what science fiction writers call a parallel world, one very much like our own but in which many or most contributors to Wikipedia are confused, error-prone, partisan, or eager to engage in vandalism. Here the wrongdoers would triumph, creating error and confusion or worse. The good-faith contributors would be overwhelmed. Nor is this world entirely hypothetical. Some wikis have run into problems as a result of these very problems. In 2005, the *Los Angeles Times* announced that it would begin to run on its Web page "wikitorials," editorials that would operate as wikis, in the sense that all readers could edit them. With evident (charming? naïve?) optimism, the editors said that they were seeking "a constantly evolving collaboration among readers in a communal search for truth."[10]

The opening editorial, involving the Iraq war, was called "War and Consequences," and it was accompanied by a wikitorial titled "Dreams about War and Retribution." Readers were invited to "rewrite the editorial yourself" if they thought that something could be improved. In just two days, the wikitorial was edited more than 150 times, in a way that significantly increased its length and scope. But on the third day, the site was flooded with pornography, and the newspaper eventually lost its technological battle with the vandals. The *LATWiki Main Page* was replaced with this somewhat mournful text: "Where is the wikitorial? Unfortunately, we have had to remove this feature, at least temporarily, because a few readers were flooding the site with inappropriate material. Thanks and apologies to the thousands of people who logged on in the right spirit."[11]

Wikis and More Wikis /

This is a story of how the wiki form might go wrong. But we should not bow to pessimism, even for wikitorials. Other newspapers are running experiments in just this vein; with better protection against vandals, perhaps the experiments will work, or at least generate some interesting results. For its article on Wikipedia, *Esquire* magazine tried a creative approach: Its author, A. J. Jacobs, posted a badly written, typo-pervaded, error-filled first draft of the article on Wikipedia itself and asked Wikipedians to improve it. The draft was edited 224 times in the first twenty-four hours after it was posted, and another 149 times in the following twenty-four hours. After the article was "locked," it was published in the magazine—and it is quite excellent.[12]

In chapter 1, I mentioned dKosopedia, "the free political encyclopedia," which offers a good deal of information about political issues. At the time of the present writing, the Politics.ie wiki is both more specialized and far more advanced; it attempts to create a comprehensive resource of information relating to Irish politics, and anyone can edit it. Detailed materials can be found about the Labour Party, Sinn Fein, the Green Party, Michael Collins, and much more. Recent events are catalogued as they occur. Wikis devoted to science, in general and in particular areas, are easy to find; a general science wiki was created in 2005.[13] An entire wiki focuses on the politics of open source software adoption.[14] All are warmly invited to participate: "In keeping with the open structure and spirit of wiki collaboration, we invite you to build on this account of free and open source software politics—adding to or revising the existing accounts, branching out into new accounts of other contexts and processes, or linking to relevant external sources."[15] On Wikicities.com, it is possible to find well over three hundred wikis. Some of these involve entertainment. Wikis are devoted to *Star Trek* (as of this writing, with a disappointing lack of detail), *Star Wars* (same parenthetical), and *Lord of the Rings* (no comment!). Others involve general topics in which many people are interested, such as insurance, cancer, globalization, and genealogy (not to mention shopping).

An especially interesting wiki is the World Wind Wiki.[16] On this site, it is possible to "zoom from outer space to any place on earth. World Wind leverages satellite imagery and elevation data to allow users to experience Earth terrain in visually rich 3D, just as if they were really there. Virtually visit anyplace in the world. Look across the Andes, into the Grand Canyon, over the Alps or along the African Sahara." Numerous users add relevant information, allowing the site to accumulate new facts and data. Lawrence Lessig has posted his influential 2000 book, *Code, and Other Laws of Cyberspace*, as a wiki, and a number of changes have been made.

Some of the most promising efforts are building directly on the Wikipedia model. Wikipedia itself has a range of sister projects, including Wikispecies (a directory of species), Wiktionary (a dictionary and thesaurus), Wikisource (a collection of primary source documents that anyone can edit), and Meta-Wiki (a Web site about the various projects of the Wikimedia Foundation). There are countless other possibilities in this vein. For example, many people have been concerned about the risk of a flu epidemic. State-of-the-art information can be found at Flu Wiki, a Web site that anyone can edit. Flu Wiki offers articles about prevention, diagnosis, treatment, and much more. As of this writing, a Flu Wiki can be found not only in English, but also in French, Spanish, and Turkish.

As an especially colorful example of the same basic form, consider the Urban Dictionary. The Urban Dictionary defines itself as "a slang dictionary with your definitions." There is no deliberation here, but it operates as a wiki; anyone can add or edit the existing definitions. The word "cool," for example, has fifty-eight definitions (as of September 2005), from the not terribly exciting "cold or having an overall cold temperature" to the somewhat better "laid back, relaxed, not freaked out, knows what's goin on." For its part, the word "cold" has, as one of its definitions, "more than cute and more than sexy its kind of like calling someone a dime." The word "dime" (for those who are puzzled and really want to know) has forty-seven definitions of its own. I won't test the reader's patience, or moral commitments, with further details. But for those who are interested in contemporary American slang, the Urban Dictionary actually provides an excellent place to start (and usually to end). It does so precisely because it aggregates highly dispersed information, as a slang dictionary should.

As a promising variation on the idea that anyone can edit, consider ohmynews.com, an online newspaper that wants to make "every citizen a reporter." The paper was founded by Oh Yeon Ho, a Korean who sought to transform what he called the "closed and elite journalistic culture." Frustrated by that culture, he created a new forum, in which anyone could submit articles. As of late 2005, ohmynews.com had a professional staff of seventy-five people, including forty-five reporters, and an official "staff" of thirty-nine thousand citizen reporters! Every day, more than two hundred articles are submitted to ohmynews.com, and about 70 percent of the submissions are published. Writers receive a small, nominal payment. As in the case of Wikipedia, people contribute for nonmaterial reasons. Unlike in the case of Wikipedia, the professional staff imposes filters, designed to ensure decent writing and accuracy. But the advantage of ohmynews.com is that it invites everyone to contribute, and in that sense promises to provide a wide range of information.

In Korea, ohmynews.com has had a substantial effect on some political disputes, and its English edition is now flourishing. It counts as a genuine success. We might expect many more ventures in this vein.

Many businesses are now using wikis. E-mail can be time-consuming and cumbersome. It is often much better to create a wiki, producing a document that anyone can edit. Walt Disney, Eastman Kodak, Yahoo, Oxford University Press, and parts of the U.S. military have used private workspace wikis, in which employees can discuss one another's work and also make immediate editorial changes in documents.[17] An artificial intelligence company, Soar Technology Inc., which works for the Office of Naval Research, reports that wikis cut the time required to finish projects by 50 percent. Some people project that in the next five years, wikis will be used by most businesses in the United States.

The quality of the wiki form is immensely variable. It will be exceptionally interesting to see how the form evolves over time. We could easily imagine amplification of errors, hidden profiles, cascade effects, and group polarization on wikis and their cousins (not excluding ohmynews.com and wikitorials). But my hunch is that the diversity of views, along with a widespread desire to cooperate, will ensure many successes, especially but not only within working groups. Of course, many experiments fail. But the explosive growth of Wikipedia, and of wikis in general, suggests that more and even better developments are on the way.

/ Open Source Software /

Now let us turn to one of the most fascinating developments in modern technology: the rise of free and open source software, often referred to as F/OSS or FOSS.[18] (For the sake of simplicity, I shall refer to "open source software," though the term is controversial for reasons we shall explore.) Much of my discussion focuses on computer code, but the potential applications are limitless. As we shall see, the very idea of "open source" can be used in domains that have nothing to do with software. Biotechnology, for example, can be open source, too. Medical research might rely less on patents; there is an active movement toward "open source medicine," in an effort to develop patent-free drugs.[19] Music too can be open source. Consider Woody Guthrie's copyright notice: "This song is Copyrighted in U.S., under Seal of Copyright # 154085, for a period of 28 years, and anybody caught singin it without our permission, will be mighty good friends of ourn, cause we don't give a dern. Publish it. Write it. Sing it. Swing to it. Yodel it. We wrote it, that's all we wanted to do."[20]

But let us begin with the general concept.

Open Source in General /

In ordinary enterprises, companies own the intellectual property that their employees produce. Microsoft, for example, has developed a great deal of original material, including computer code, which is owned by Microsoft and kept private. So, too, famously and long before, with Coca-

Cola, which owns the formula for making its product and which keeps that formula a secret entirely unavailable to the public. Within companies, intense deliberation occurs in the effort to develop more and better information and products; certainly this is true at Microsoft and also at Google. Ordinary people are often denied access to that information.

In an economy that protects private property, it is standard for both individuals and companies to refuse to disclose valuable knowledge. Patent and copyright law explicitly protects the right to hold information in private hands, precisely to encourage innovation. The legitimate concern here is that if many minds have free access to information, less information will be generated in the first place. If anyone can own a book or an invention, there might well be fewer good books and fewer beneficial inventions. Economic incentives frequently work, and if those incentives are removed, many people will not produce desirable products, and society will be much poorer and more ignorant as a result. In any case, much information, and much computer code, does turn out to be "proprietary," in the sense that those who have it keep it to themselves.

In contrast to proprietary projects, open source projects ensure that the original source material (or code) is freely available to others who use it. The whole idea is to ensure access by many minds. Perhaps improvements will be more likely, and more rapid, if the code is open to all users. On this view, open source software has a built-in advantage over proprietary software, just as Wikipedia has an advantage over Nupedia. In the illuminating words of Lawrence Lessig, "Proprietary software is like Kentucky Fried Chicken. Open source and free software is like Kentucky Fried Chicken sold with the 'original secret recipe' printed in bold on the box."[21] Or return to the Coca-Cola example: You cannot have access to Coca-Cola's formula so as to make improvements. But believe it or not, there is now open source cola, OpenCola, which you can find at opencola.org (complete with a full account of ingredients; you're entirely welcome to make improvements if you like).

As the example reveals, the most important characteristic of open source projects is that they permit their users to change them and to make them better. (Woody Guthrie well understood this point with respect to folk music, and Bob Dylan proved him right.) Users can certainly deliberate with one another, but it is also possible to work entirely on one's own and then to communicate the solution, or improvement, that one has found. My concern here is with the use of open source methods to aggregate dispersed information and to incorporate dispersed creativity; but by way of background, we should explore a few technicalities.

Provisos, Conditions, and Copyleft /
Open source software often comes with an important proviso, which is that those who use the material must agree that they will make their improvements available to anyone else under the same conditions. In this sense, open source software is deliberately available to, and can be improved by, many minds. Notably, such software is always "free" in one sense but sometimes not in another. It is always free in the same sense that free speech is free; it is not held privately by identifiable people. The code is available for all users to see. Open source software is also free in the important sense that people can *sell* it. At the same time, you might well have to pay to get it. Open source software is protected by copyright, which is one reason that various conditions can be attached to it. Such software is not in the public domain. In this sense, most open source and free software are the same as

Wikipedia, which is also protected by a copyright license—more particularly, it is "copylefted," a concept to which I now turn.

It is important to distinguish between open source software that is copylefted, in the sense that stringent (but public-friendly) conditions are attached to it, and open source software that is not. In Lessig's words, copylefted software "is licensed under terms that require follow-on users to require others to adopt the same license terms for work derived from the copylefted code. The principle is 'share and share alike.'"[22] Under this approach, the sharing principle is mandatory; people are not free to reject it.

The purpose of copyleft licenses is to ensure that open source programs remain open source when a third party redistributes the program or a derivative work. There are strong and weak versions of copyleft. The strong version requires that any subsequent derived work must apply the original copyleft version to the whole work, including any sections authored entirely by the subsequent programmer. The most common strong copyleft license, the General Public License (GPL), provides that "when you distribute the [independently authored] sections as part of a whole which is a work based on the Program, the distribution of the whole must be on the terms of this License."[23] This provision of the GPL makes it exceedingly difficult for proprietary software developers to use open source software governed by the GPL anywhere in their code—which indeed is the goal.[24]

The weak version of copyleft differs in one important respect: Independently authored components distributed with the open source code can be separately licensed. That is, whereas the original code and modified versions of it must retain the weak copyleft license, separately authored components are allowed to have distinct (i.e., more restrictive or proprietary) licensing provisions.[25] If code is not copylefted at all, conditions of this kind are not imposed on later use. If people want to redistribute modified versions of the code they purchased, they are permitted to do so on whatever terms they choose. The popular Apache Web Server is open source software that is not copylefted. The popular GNU/Linux operating system is copylefted.

The most general point is that open source software provides a method by which decentralized bits of private knowledge and creativity can be elicited and used. Contributions are possible from anyone who can help. As a result, it is possible to obtain improvements that may well go far beyond the capacities of small groups of experts. With open source software, expert groups may and do deliberate about improvements. But in addition, numerous contributors can bring their own imagination and knowledge to bear. Some of these contributors work on their own; others work in teams. The important fact is that countless people can make improvements—and they do, sometimes for economic reasons, sometimes not.

Those who celebrate open source software, and believe that it has major advantages over alternative methods, emphasize this point above all. Note here Eric Raymond's suggestion: "Given enough eyeballs, all bugs are shallow."[26]

A Movement /

Open source software has an extremely colorful history; it even involves a kind of social movement, with vivid personalities and a great deal of passion and commitment.[27] The Free Software Foundation, a nonprofit organization, was started by Richard Stallman in 1985, the same year that Stallman invented the copyleft license; and Stallman, to whom I shall return, has been a foundational figure for over two decades. An important moment in the movement occurred in 1991, when Linus Torvalds, a computer science graduate student at the University of Helsinki, started to do some interesting work on his personal computer. Torvalds was adding features to Minix, a miniaturized version of the operating system Unix; Minix had been written for pedagogical purposes by programmer Andrew Tanenbaum. Minix had not been freely licensed, a point that helped persuade Torvalds to build his own version. After a period of work, Torvalds released the source code for his operating system, which he named Linux, onto an Internet newsgroup. He appended an informal and now famous note:

> I'm working on a free version. . . . It has finally reached the stage where it's even usable (though may not be depending on what you want), and I am willing to put out the sources for wider distribution. . . . This is a program for hackers by a hacker. I've enjoyed doing it, and somebody might enjoy looking at it and even modifying it for their own needs. It is still small enough to understand, use and modify, and I'm looking forward to any comments you might have. . . . I'd like to hear from you so I can add them to the system. . . . PS. to PHIL NELSON! I'm unable to get through to you, and keep getting "forward error—strawberry unknown domain" or something.[28]

Torvalds received a large and enthusiastic response, allowing him to improve the system markedly. In the 1990s, Linux steadily grew in quality, and by 2000, it had become a phenomenal success in the market. "A hugely complex and sophisticated operating system had been built out of the voluntary contributions of thousands of developers spread around the world. By the middle of 2000, Linux ran more than a third of the servers that make up the web."[29] As of this writing, only about 2 percent of the Linux "kernel," or core, is written by Torvalds himself, but he continues to exercise ultimate authority over the decision whether to incorporate new code.[30]

I have referred to Richard Stallman, a famous hacker and near celebrity who originated the GNU project; GNU is a free software operating system for which Stallman wrote the GNU General Public License, now the most public free software license. With his multiple achievements, Stallman has become a legendary figure within the movement. (Personal note: I went to college with Stallman in the mid-1970s and lived in the same dormitory with him. He was well-known as a brilliant, eccentric, and extremely intense person and as someone who was quite focused on computers. As it happens, Bill Gates spent some time in the same dormitory; he was not eccentric, as I recall, and he was not particularly intense, but he also liked computers.) Stallman's interest in free software began in the 1980s, when he rejected proprietary software and nondisclosure principles on the theory that hackers should be free to make changes as they saw fit. As he describes the situation at that time, his "easy choice was to join the proprietary software world, signing nondisclosure agreements and promising not to help my fellow hacker. Most likely I would also be developing software that was released under nondisclosure agreements, thus adding to the pressure on other people to betray their fellows too."[31] Stallman thus took steps to promote software that would "give users freedom" by allowing them to see and to modify source code.

Stallman much prefers the term "free software" to "open source software," arguing that the latter term does not show the connection with liberty: "The English language has more words and nuances than any other, but it lacks a simple, unambiguous word that means 'free,' as in freedom— 'unfettered' being the word that comes closest in meaning."[32] Freedom, rather than information aggregation, is Stallman's emphasis. His preferred term appears not to have won, largely on the theory that "open" is a less confusing way to refer to products that are, after all, bought and sold. (The term F/OSS, for free/open source software, now has considerable currency; FLOSS, a term that Stallman accepts and that includes "software libre," is the preferred and perhaps politically correct term in Brazil and some European communities.) Whatever the best term, there is no question that Stallman's basic project continues to gain ground in the world of software and elsewhere.

It is clear that open source software has been a substantial economic success. Apache, an open source project, has dominated the market for server software since 1995. According to a recent analysis, about 70 percent of servers use Apache or other open source products, and thus reject the proprietary products offered by Sun, Microsoft, and others.[33] Linux accounts for a substantial percentage of the operating systems of all servers, and it has a larger market share than Microsoft as the operating system most often used in video recording devices and mobile phones. In many other areas, open source products are in widespread use.[34]

Notwithstanding all this, there is some dispute about whether the strongest open source enthusiasts have overstated their case. In desktop environments, for example, Windows and MacOSX do much better than the open source alternatives. But no one doubts that open source has done exceedingly well. Why is this? And what lessons can be drawn from the answer to this question for deliberation and information aggregation in general?

Cathedrals and Bazaars /

In a famous and illuminating essay, programmer Eric Raymond distinguished between two models of production: the cathedral and the bazaar.[35] On one view, which Raymond himself initially accepted, computer software should be built in the fashion of cathedrals, which are carefully planned in advance, on the basis of specific judgments emerging from individuals or small groups. (The Soviet Union tried to run its economy in cathedral-like fashion, with its careful but doomed five-year plans.) On the alternative account, software development should not be based on "quiet, reverent cathedral-building," but instead come from "a great babbling bazaar of differing agendas and approaches . . . out of which a coherent and stable system could seemingly emerge only by a succession of miracles."[36]

Nonetheless, the miracles occurred. In fact, they continue to appear every day. In Hayekian fashion, we can see many human institutions, including language, culture, and even law, as products of a bazaar rather than of any self-conscious process of cathedral-like design. Bazaars reflect a kind of spontaneous order. They are best understood as a mechanism for ensuring that widely dispersed knowledge is captured in human products.

But when will bazaars work? It is one thing to emphasize the price system, which creates material incentives for disclosure of information. It is quite another thing to emphasize the use of bazaars to create computer code. From the standpoint of conventional economists, the success of open source software remains a bit of a puzzle. The problem is that some contributors appear to have no incentive to make improvements. In most markets, those who create or improve a product are likely to make money; the profit motive is the great impetus for innovation. Or so it is thought. But for open source software, some of those who make changes receive no economic reward. Tens of thousands of people, from all over the world, have been willing to contribute to open source software, and they have done so without gaining a dollar.

There are interesting complications here. Much work performed on open source projects, especially major ones, is carried out by programmers who work at big firms, such as Hewlett Packard and IBM. These programmers hardly work for free. On the contrary, they are compensated for their labor by employers who want to ensure that high-quality open source software is available, with the company selling support services and hardware.[37] But it remains true that many programmers do not receive direct compensation at all.

Is this a truly Hayekian process, to be explained directly in Hayek's terms? The answer is both yes and no. Yes, in the sense that open source software benefits from the inclusion of countless bits of information from widely dispersed people with diverse knowledge and tastes. No, in the sense that financial incentives are not always responsible for people's behavior. But when the profit motive is absent, why do people contribute? Some people act out of a simple commitment to the enterprise of innovation. Others are devoted to the idea of open source as such, connecting it with freedom and democracy; they participate for that very reason. Some contributors greatly enjoy spending their time writing code. Others are genuine altruists, hoping to benefit others. Raymond himself contends that the world of hackers is a "gift culture" as distinguished from an "exchange culture"; in this gift culture, "social status is determined not by what you control but *by what you give away*." Thus, "participants compete for prestige by giving time, energy, and creativity away."[38]

This point suggests that status motives, rather than altruism, are playing the key role. Many contributors undoubtedly have a desire for approval or even glory, or perhaps the more quiet sense of individual satisfaction that comes from an innovation. (Recall Wikipedia, to which many people contribute from a similar motivation.) In Raymond's words, "One's work is one's statement."[39] In addition, status may also create at least a prospect of economic benefits: Those who contribute a great deal might be able to get better employment as a result.

There is a further point. Participants, even peripheral ones, use an important tool, and they want it to work as well as it possibly can. When they report a problem, they increase the likelihood that it will be fixed, and they stand to benefit for that reason. What is most noteworthy is that for many people, the process works well, with and without a clear economic spur.

As in the case of Wikipedia, the analogy to the price signal is strained. To be sure, the code now found in open source software is an aggregation of dispersed bits of information; but it is not a price. Those who make changes and improvements sometimes respond to economic incentives, direct or indirect. But they are not consumers, motivated purely by financial incentives and adding their own preferences to the mix.

Governance and Filters /
Some open source software projects typically have no formal process of governance; their small size allows everything to work by consensus.[40] For larger projects, the improvement process contains "filters" that go well beyond those in Wikipedia. In this sense, Wikipedia's "last in time" model, in which the final editor can make numerous changes, is very

different from, and far less constrained than, the open source process, which usually depends on some kind of hierarchical arrangement. Here, then, are some distinctive models for aggregating dispersed information.

Participants in development projects are frequently divided into the core and the periphery. The periphery includes ordinary users who are able to test products and to identify problems. The core includes leaders with overall responsibility; many of them help to code the initial release of the software, and they are in charge of the direction of projects. Deliberative processes within the core play a key role; recall that when eureka-type problems are involved, such processes are likely to work. The Mozilla community, for example, has a highly successful open source program, and it maintains itself through an interesting combination of formality and informality, supported by the Mozilla Foundation.[41] The organization includes staff, drivers, module owners, peers, super-reviewers, developers, and others.

Mozilla's code solicitation process is well developed. Simple contributions can be made by using a developmental version of the program and by reporting problems or "bugs" that are encountered. The community uses a program called Bugzilla to centralize information about known problems. After users and developers have identified problems and areas for improvement, interested developers can begin work. Such development takes place at an exceptionally rapid rate. For example, between midnight and 7:30 a.m. on July 20, 2005, eighteen changes were "checked in" (introduced into the main version) by nine different people with access to the code. At least four additional programmers created or contributed to these changes, which provided such benefits as enabling Chinese newsgroups to function properly in the Web browser.[42]

Before such improvements can be incorporated into the source code repository, they must be screened in a two-step process. Once a developer has completed a patch, she can post it on Bugzilla linked to the appropriate bug listing and request review. The reviewer checks the code to ensure that it does what it is supposed to do and sometimes provides comments that must be addressed before approval. After initial review, the developer must seek a second level of review. After approval, Bugzilla will reflect the fact that the code has been successfully reviewed and can be checked into the repository by anyone with access to it.

Linux has also adopted a relatively formal process for approving changes. That process involves layers of decisions in a kind of pyramidal structure containing a significant amount of deliberation. Ultimately, improvements have to be approved by an expert committee. "Torvalds sits atop the pyramid as essentially a benevolent dictator with final responsibility for managing decisions that cannot be resolved at lower levels."[43] Numerous people are permitted to offer suggestions, but they are not incorporated into the software unless approved through the governance structure.

Apache has developed its own distinctive approach. It began in 1995 with just eight people. After a short period, it grew to contain a few dozen members of the development core, along with several hundred other people who added ideas and suggestions. The core included people in a number of countries, including the United States, Canada, Germany, Italy, and Britain. Originally decisions could be made by consensus, produced by a deliberative process with informal e-mail exchanges. But as the group of participants grew, more formality was required. Ultimately Apache adopted a system of e-mail voting, with complex rules designed to ensure consensus within the Apache Group, itself chosen by a system of peer review. Deliberation is emphatically involved. On one view, "the Apache consensus procedure is not perfect; it seems to work less well during periods of rapid, intense development than for incremental change."[44] In 1999, the Apache Software Foundation, a nonprofit corporation, replaced the Apache Group; it operates as an umbrella for many open source projects with their own management committees.

The Open Future of Open Source /

Whatever the particular structure, the general point here is simple: With open source software, there is no unitary or publicly available good that anyone can edit. On this count, wikis offers a radically different model. Undoubtedly, the existence of layers and filters slows down the rate at which improvements can be made. But the process, containing deliberation at key points, nonetheless means that anyone with a good idea is likely to be able to improve the operation of the software.

With open source software, dispersed knowledge and creativity can easily be brought to bear. It is for this reason, above all, that open source has proved so successful in practice—and that the open source model has inspired people's interest outside of the context of computer code, for example, with biotechnology and medicine. Often the law permits people to "close" their sources, as through patents that keep processes private. On one view, this process is necessary to ensure the right incentives. If drug companies can patent their products, it is more likely that they will develop beneficial medicines. But on another view, release of the relevant data can spur innovation as well as broaden distribution. "Goodwill, aggregated over the Internet," might serve to "produce good medicine."[45]

Open source projects come in many forms. Considerable attention is now being given to open source biotechnology, by which research in agricultural and medical biotechnology is run on open source principles, with the goal of increasing innovation in this crucial area.[46] Consider, for example, the question of genetic modification of plants. Some methods of genetic modification are protected by patents, and it can be complex, difficult, and expensive to obtain licenses. Moreover, the patent system threatens to stifle innovation simply because it restricts information to the few. In the words of one critic, "When there are dozens or hundreds of patents involved, negotiations can be labyrinthine—and all it takes is one denied right to stop the whole process."[47] But scientists have recently developed an open source technique for genetic engineering, one that is not controlled by the patent system. Scientists "are free to use the technique without commercial restrictions, but must share any improvements they make to this scientific 'toolkit.'"[48]

Life is full of good coincidences. Here is one: A coauthor of the key paper on this problem, Dr. Richard Jefferson, is a descendent of Thomas Jefferson, the famous defender of democracy and openness. Dr. Jefferson says, "I see this as unfinished family business." He emphasizes that his goal is to harness "the latent creativity of a very large number of people who are out of the loop right now."[49] Biological Innovation for Open Society, or BIOS, is now attempting to increase openness in biological science. Users of open source biology own the patents to their creations, but they cannot ban other people from using the original shared information to produce other products. In addition, they must inform the public of any improvements in the methods of BIOS, and also of any health problems that are discovered. In these ways, open source biology ensures far more openness than does the patent system.

To be sure, patents are awarded to increase innovation, and it is not clear that open source projects are better on that count. In the end, the question how best to promote innovation is an empirical one. Much will depend on whether the complex set of motivations that have worked for open source software will work for other products as well. The central point is that it is possible to give numerous minds access to certain processes, and that in some circumstances, at least, this access is an engine for rapid improvements. As in the cases of wikis, we will undoubtedly find many surprises here, and they are likely to be good ones. With open source projects, human creativity will continue to ensure exciting and even barely imaginable innovations.

A Brief Note on Copyright /
There is an obvious relationship between the ideas that underlie open source software and the broader debates over the restrictions imposed by the copyright laws.[50] The whole idea of copyleft, invented by Richard Stallman, is an effort to reduce people's ability to limit the distribution and modification of software. We could easily imagine more general efforts to reduce the effects of the copyright laws; such efforts are in fact easy to find.

Copyright laws create monopolies; they diminish access by many minds. As in the context of software, legal restrictions may also spur innovation; if copyright restrictions are available, perhaps more people will produce valuable work in the first place. But it is not always clear whether we will receive more, or less, in the way of creativity with such restrictions. I have referred to the Creative Commons

License, pioneered by Lawrence Lessig, founder of the Creative Commons. A major goal of this license is to promote greater distribution of copyrighted works by allowing copyright holders to impose certain restrictions while also allowing free distribution. If holders of a Creative Commons License choose, they can forbid alteration of the underlying material; they can also restrict free copying to noncommercial uses. License holders have a range of possible options. The key point is that with the Creative Commons License, people are much freer to copy and distribute the underlying work.

A number of record labels now use the Creative Commons License, and various books, including Eric Raymond's *The Cathedral and the Bazaar,* do so as well. Lessig's own book, *Free Culture,* was released on the Internet under a Creative Commons License. The day after its online release, a popular blogger suggested that people should pick a chapter and make a voice recording of it, a process that was completed in a few days. (The book was rapidly translated into Chinese—by a wiki system.) As I have also mentioned, Wikipedia operates under the GNU Free Documentation License, which was originally intended for software but similarly can be used broadly to promote access by many minds.

With greater freedom to copy and to distribute, we should expect a dramatic increase in creativity in multiple domains. But as we shall now see, creativity, even amid many minds, can also offer some highly ambivalent lessons.

/ Blogs /

One of the most unanticipated developments of the first years of the twenty-first century was the remarkable rise of Weblogs, which can serve to elicit and aggregate the information held by countless contributors. Weblogs, or blogs, have been growing at a truly astounding rate, so much so that any current account will rapidly grow out of date. At the present time, more than 50 million blogs are up and running. Tens of thousands blogs are created each day, with a new one every 2.2 seconds. (Question: How many blogs are created in the time it takes to read a short book?) In recent years, the most highly rated political blogs—including Atrios, Instapundit, and Daily Kos—have received at least several tens of thousands of visitors *each day*. The worlds of law and politics are full of blogs, and my own institution, the University of Chicago Law School, has its own Faculty Blog, dealing (most of the time) with questions of law.

Stories /
Every well-known blog has its own story, often full of some combination of talent, luck, and coincidence. Consider Instapundit, run by Glenn Reynolds, a professor of law at the University of Tennessee. Before becoming a blogger, Reynolds was a moderately well-known law professor with several strong publications. On August 8, 2001, he began Instapundit, in part inspired by his Internet law class.[51] Since that point, his blog has grown into one of the largest on the Internet, attracting more than one hundred thousand visits per day. As a result of his remarkable success, Reynolds is sometimes referred to as "the Blogfather."

Reynolds provides commentary of varied length, sometimes merely linking to an interesting story or post found elsewhere, and sometimes explaining his own point of view at length. His own views are eclectic. He has also expanded into the mainstream, blogging at GlennReynolds.com for MSNBC, and his writings have appeared in many traditional outlets, including the *Washington Post* and the *Wall Street Journal*; he also writes regularly for the Fox News Web site. (Full disclosure: Reynolds invited me to post on his site on msnbc.com for a week in 2004, and it was astounding to receive the range of e-mail responses, by turns smart, funny, enraged, helpful, nutty, and incoherent.)

Blog Triumphalism? /

Bloggers have occasionally had an impact on real-world events, and their impact may be growing. Drawing from the account of blogging enthusiast Hugh Hewitt,[52] let us consider a few examples:

- Bloggers deserve significant credit for the 2004 "Rather-gate" scandal, in which Dan Rather used what seemed to be authentic memoranda to offer embarrassing disclosures about the military service of President George W. Bush. The memoranda indicated that Bush had failed to do his duty, and indeed had refused to obey direct orders. Careful bloggers showed that the memoranda could not possibly be authentic. Only one day after the broadcast, a blogger known as Buckhead wrote, "Every single one of these memos to file is in a proportionally spaced font, probably Palatino or Times New Roman. In 1972 people used typewriters for this sort of thing, and typewriters used monospaced fonts. . . . I am saying these documents are forgeries, run through a copier for 15 generations to make them look old." Additional bloggers worked hard to confirm the accusation. As Hewitt notes, bloggers "exposed the fraud with breathtaking speed and finality."[53]
- In 2002, Trent Lott, Senate majority leader, spoke at a birthday party for Senator Strom Thurmond. Lott said of Mississippi, his own state, "When Strom Thurmond ran

for president, we voted for him. We're proud of it. And if the rest of the country had followed our lead, we wouldn't have had all these problems over all these years, either." This was a genuinely scandalous statement; Thurmond had run on a racist, pro-segregation platform, and the Senate majority leader seemed to be saying that if Thurmond had won, the nation would have been problem-free. But somehow the remarks were ignored—except on the blogosphere. A blogger named Atrios gave serious coverage to the comments, which were then picked up on talkingpointsmemo.com, and the building momentum proved unstoppable. Lott was forced to resign as majority leader.

■ In 1979, John Kerry said, "I remember spending Christmas Eve of 1968 five miles across the Cambodian border being shot at by our South Vietnamese allies who were drunk and celebrating Christmas." In the 2004 election, the blogosphere was full of stories about whether Kerry had really spent Christmas Eve in Cambodia, and indeed whether he had been in Cambodia at all. The doubts raised questions about the credibility of Kerry's statements about his record in the Vietnam War. Focusing on the claim of Christmas Eve in Cambodia, one blogger, RogerLSimon.com, objected to the prospect of having someone "who sounds like a pathetic barroom blowhard" as president of the United States, especially "in a time of war. People like this start to believe their own lies." A liberal blogger, Matthew Yglesias, said, "It certainly looks bad from here, and I haven't seen a good explanation yet, perhaps because there isn't one." Eventually, the Kerry campaign acknowledged that Kerry had not been in Cambodia on Christmas in 1968. Hewitt writes, "The Christmas-Eve-not-in-Cambodia became shorthand for

Kerry's fantasy life, and suddenly the Swift Vets" who savagely attacked Kerry's honesty and patriotism "had credibility, as Internet donations flowed into their coffers."[54]

Whatever one thinks of these events, bloggers appear to have influenced the public stage, driving media coverage and affecting national perceptions of national questions. And of course, there is much more. In my own area of law, bloggers offer quick and insightful analyses of legal events. Those analyses are widely read, and they can influence media coverage as well. When bloggers err on legal questions, their errors are often corrected. To take just one example: The Volokh Conspiracy, an extremely popular law-related Web site, often provides discussions of important Supreme Court decisions, sometimes on the day those decisions are announced. These discussions put the Court's decisions in context and typically provide illuminating criticisms. If the analysis seems to go wrong, the author is immediately notified, and a correction or debate usually ensues. Other events in law and politics often receive instructive and immediate attention.

In law and policy more broadly, Nobel Prize winner Gary Becker and court of appeals judge Richard A. Posner have run a blog (named, not so imaginatively, the Becker-Posner blog) that offers substantive discussions of such issues as global warming, property rights, health insurance, terrorism, and bankruptcy reform. Becker and Posner receive thousands of visitors each week, and those visitors offer insightful comments and corrections.

Of course, there is a great deal more. Bloggers frequently deliberate with one another, exchanging information and perspectives. Becker and Posner regularly feature debates between the two. The Volokh Conspiracy is run by law professor Eugene Volokh, but it has a number of contributors with different perspectives. Disagreement among the contributors is common; a debate on same-sex marriage or the future of the Supreme Court is far from unusual. Discussion and argument occur every day across blogs, not just within them. Because of their openness, speed, and flexibility, some people believe that blogs will come to replace, at least in part, the discussions of law and politics that can now be found in traditional academic journals. The very fact that an analysis can be done in an hour or a day might seem to make such journals obsolete.

In addition, many blogs offer public space for comments by anyone who cares to participate. If a blogger makes an error, or merely appears to make an error, there is a good chance that someone will complain. Often the comment sections take on lives of their own, offering vigorous debates on topics only lightly explored by the post that inspired them. In the University of Chicago Law School, one of the most interesting developments is the extensive use of the comment section, in which people often engage with one another, and not so much with the post that originally triggered their exchange.

Indeed, the blogosphere might be seen as a kind of gigantic town meeting, or series of such meetings. The presence of many minds is especially important here. If countless people are maintaining their own blogs, they should be able to act as fact-checkers and as supplemental information sources, not only for one another but also for prominent members of the mass media. If hundreds of thousands of people are reading the most prominent blogs, then errors should be corrected quickly. In addition, the blogosphere enables interested readers to find an astounding range of opinions and facts. Judge Posner has gone so far as to invoke Hayek's argument about the price system on behalf of blogs, emphasizing their potential to reveal dispersed bits of information. In Judge Posner's words:

> Blogging is . . . a fresh and striking exemplification of Friedrich Hayek's thesis that knowledge is widely distributed among people and that the challenge to society is to create mechanisms for pooling that knowledge. The powerful mechanism that was the focus of Hayek's work, as of economists generally, is the price system (the market). The newest mechanism is the "blogosphere." There are 4 million blogs. The Internet enables the instantaneous pooling (and hence correction, refinement, and amplification) of the ideas and opinions, facts and images, reportage and scholarship, generated by bloggers.[55]

Not Hayek: Problems in the Blogosphere /
But Judge Posner's use of Hayek misses the mark, and we should therefore resist blog triumphalism. Indeed, the very problems that infect deliberation can be found on the blogosphere, too. The world of blogs is pervaded by the propagation of errors, hidden profiles, cascades, and group polarization.

Even the best blogs lack anything like prepublication peer review, and their speed and informality often ensure glibness, superficiality, confusion, and blatant errors. Many blogs in law and politics are close to talk radio, or to brisk and irresponsible conversations over the lunch table. (Granted, that is part of what makes them fun.) Sometimes falsehoods spread like wildfire, as informational and reputational cascades lead to widespread mistakes. Confidently stated errors have proliferated on countless topics, including the plans of Israel and Iran, the likely Supreme Court nominees of President George W. Bush, and the political views (and corruption, or worse) of both Republicans and Democrats. Group polarization is easy to find on blogs; the conservative-leaning Volokh Conspiracy, despite its civility, intelligence, and overall high quality, is an occasional example, with commentators sometimes leading one another to more extreme versions of what they thought before discussions began.

The blogosphere does not produce prices, which aggregate, in one place, a wide range of opinions and tastes. It certainly does not work as open source software does. It does not produce a giant wiki, aggregating dispersed information. Instead, it offers a stunningly diverse range of claims, perspectives, rants, insights, lies, facts, falsehood, sense, and nonsense.

Participants in the blogospere usually lack an economic incentive. They are not involved in any kind of trade, and most of the time they have little to gain or to lose. If they spread falsehoods, or simply offer their opinion, they do not sacrifice a thing. Perhaps their reputation will suffer, but perhaps not; perhaps the most dramatic falsehoods will draw attention and hence readers. Most bloggers do not have the economic stake of those who trade on prediction markets. True, some bloggers attract advertising, and many blogs aggregate a lot of information; instapundit.com, for example, assembles material from many sources. But it is not possible to find a Superblog, in general or in particular areas, that corresponds to Wikipedia or open source software. In other words, we lack a blog that succeeds in correcting errors and assembling truths. Those who consult blogs will learn a great deal, but they will have an exceedingly hard time separating falsehoods from facts.

By their very nature, blogs offer rival and contentious positions on facts as well as values. In many ways, this is a virtue, for people who are curious can find a wide range of views, including those that oppose their own. But if truth is to emerge, it is because of the competition of the marketplace of ideas, and the discussion thus far suggests that this particular marketplace is far from reliable. One of the undeniable effects of blogs is to spread misunderstandings and mistakes. If deliberating groups propagate error and leave hidden profiles, we can be sure that those who write or read blogs will do the same thing.

To return to one of my primary themes: A particular problem arises if people are reading blogs that conform to their own preexisting beliefs. If this is so, polarization is inevitable. Liberals reading liberal blogs will end up more liberal; conservatives will become more conservative if they restrict themselves to conservative blogs. The Colorado experiment, involving group polarization, finds itself replicated in the blogosphere every day, with potentially harmful results. People sometimes go to extremes simply because they are consulting others who think as they do. The rise of blogs makes it all the easier for people to live in echo chambers of their own design. Indeed, some bloggers, and many readers of blogs, live in information cocoons.

Can anything be done about this? Here's one idea: Public-spirited bloggers would do well to offer links to those whose views are quite different from their own. Liberal blogs could more regularly link to conservative ones, and vice versa. We could easily imagine explicit or implicit "deals" among bloggers with competing opinions, producing mutual linking. Such deals would increase the likelihood that people will be exposed to different perspectives; they would also reflect a healthy degree of mutual respect.

Of course, blogs do add to the range of available views, and they certainly hold out the promise of aggregating information held by large numbers of people. As Posner suggests, blogging could operate as an extraodinary method for collecting dispersed knowledge. Sheer numbers could and do play a large and beneficial role here, because information aggregation is likely to work best when many minds are involved; but it is also important that reasons and information are being exchanged in a way that can lead to corrections and real creativity. To some extent, this is happening already. But whereas the price system automatically collects dispersed information, and open source software contains a remarkable system for aggregating with filters, and Wikipedia provides an aggregating mechanism with both formal and informal safeguards, blogs offer no filters, and the only safeguards come from the discipline of the market for ideas.

Evidence /

What do we actually know about the blogosphere? All too little. The empirical analysis remains in its earliest stages. But there is good evidence that many bloggers are mostly linking to like-minded others, and that when they link to opinions that diverge from their own, it is often to cast ridicule and scorn on them.

One study explores the degree to which conservative and liberal bloggers are interacting with each other. Focusing on fourteen hundred blogs, the study finds that 91 percent of the links are to like-minded sites.[56] Hence, the two sides sort themselves into identifiable communities. For example, powerlineblog.com, a conservative blog, is linked to by only twenty-five liberal blogs, but by 195 conservative blogs. Dailykos.com, a liberal blog, is linked to by forty-six conservative blogs, but by 292 liberal blogs. In the aggregate, the behavior of conservative bloggers is more noteworthy in this regard; they link to one another far more often and in a denser pattern.

The study's authors also examined about forty "A-List" blogs, and here, too, they found a great deal of segregation. Sources were cited almost exclusively by one side or the other. Those sites with identifiable political commitments, such as Salon.com and NationalReview.com, were almost always cited by blogs on the same side of the political spectrum.

Another study, by Eszter Hargittai, Jason Gallo, and Matt Kane, offers more detailed support for the same general conclusions.[57] Examining the behavior of forty popular blogs, half liberal and half conservative, Hargittai and her coauthors find that like-minded views receive a great deal of reinforcement. On the "blogrolls," referring readers to other blogs, conservatives are far more likely to list other conservatives, and liberals are far more likely to list other liberals. When blogs refer to discussions by other bloggers, they usually cite like-minded others. To be sure, there is a significant amount of cross-citation as well. But—and here is perhaps the most striking finding—a significant percentage of the cross-citations simply cast contempt on the views that are being cited. In this way, real deliberation is often occurring within established points of view, not across them.

The general conclusion is that in the blogosphere, there is a significant divide among politically identifiable communities. Liberals and conservatives do not usually link to one another. Much of the time, they do not even discuss the same topics. To be sure, many people are using the blogosphere to learn about different views and new topics. Just like the Internet of which it is a part, the blogosphere increases the range of options, and this is a great virtue, above all for curious and open-minded people. On balance, the blogosphere, like the Internet more generally, is certainly good for democracy because it increases information. But if linking behavior on blogs can be taken as a proxy for information filtering, it is reasonable to think that many readers are obtaining one-sided views of political issues.

The construction of information cocoons and echo chambers is a real problem for a democracy, not least because amplification of errors, hidden profiles, cascade effects, and polarization are inevitable. For many people, blunders and extremism are highly likely, not in spite of the blogosphere but because of it.

/ Creative Futures for Many Minds /

It is possible to imagine many different efforts to aggregate dispersed information. Experiments in this vein are cropping up all the time. Consider a few of many examples.

Slashdot, the largest community-driven technology site on the Internet, has long identified itself as "news for nerds, stuff that matters." Slashdot is, among other things, an edited compilation of news abstracts, focusing on a wide range of topics related to technology. A first-time visitor to Slashdot will notice that the site resembles an ordinary news site, with story headlines, synopses, and links to follow. But its real value lies in the fact that it permits its users to discuss both news articles and one another's posts. Specifically, Slashdot users can spark discussions by posting ideas and responses to particular articles, thus facilitating discussion.

Of course, the system is vulnerable to irrelevant, silly, and abusive comments. Slashdot's ingenious response is a "moderation system," by which users judge comments and rank them by score. At first, the founders of Slashdot moderated posts themselves. But as the user base expanded, the job of moderating became unmanageable and was therefore delegated to users. As a result, a group of moderators has been selected from a pool of active users. Many minds thus evaluate the contributions of many minds.

As the system operates, all comments are scored on an absolute scale from –1 to 5. Logged-in users start at 1 (although this can vary from 0 to 2 based on their prior actions), and anonymous users start at 0. Moderators can add or deduct points from a comment's score, thus influencing whether a comment will be immediately visible to a reader. (Confession: Slashdot had a discussion of my 2001 book, *Republic.com*; as the author, I ventured a nonanonymous comment, which was ranked very low: 0, as I recall. True, I probably deserved the low ranking.)

Of course, there is a risk that the moderators will promote an agenda of their own. To combat that risk, Slashdot has produced the ingenious mechanism of "metamoderation," which operates as a review process of the moderation system. Instead of rating the usefulness of a comment, metamoderation rates the fairness and accuracy of the moderator's judgment.[58] According to the metamoderation statistics, 92 percent to 93 percent of moderations are judged fair.[59] (Hence, it is not necessary, to date, to create metametamoderation, reviewing the metamoderators!)

Slashdot explores a wide range of questions relating to technology, but more specialized aggregations, involving goods and activities of relevance to everyday life, are easy to imagine. An obvious question, of potential interest to many people, is this: How might many minds be enlisted in the evaluation of products and services? Angie's List, founded by Angie Hicks, is one attempt at an answer; it collects and distributes detailed customer satisfaction reports on local businesses in over twenty-six major cities. For a $10 sign-up fee and a $5.95 monthly charge, subscribers can find reviews of neighborhood service providers and contractors. Members are able to read what other customers are saying about a business before hiring them.

Angie's List is hardly a new concept. The Better Business Bureau has a similar service, giving companies either a satisfactory rating or listing their number of complaints. But Angie's List provides a great deal of inside information through its rating system, which gives the subscriber the most recent reports on numerous companies. There are countless analogues on the Internet, as customers evaluate a wide range of products—cars, books, and more—and allow the evaluations to be aggregated to produce useful information. (Recall the Condorcet Jury Theorem.)

There are many other methods for obtaining the evaluations of large numbers of people. Visited by millions of people every month, Rotten Tomatoes aggregates the reviews of approved critics about movies, DVDs, and video games. The site is *not* open to all reviewers: Movie reviews are posted by critics from "accredited media outlets and online film societies." Before a critic is allowed to post on the site, she must complete an application and be certified by the owners of the site that she is a bona fide movie critic.

Views are aggregated on Rotten Tomatoes through two methods: the "Tomatometer" and the "Average Rating." The Tomatometer is a measure of how highly recommended a given film is, while the Average Rating is a more precise measure of the quality of the movie. The Average Rating score is simply the average of each critic's 1–10 rating of a given film. The Tomatometer score indicates the percentage of "Approved Tomatometer Critics" who have recommended a movie. A movie is deemed to be "Fresh" if its

Tomatometer score is 60 percent or greater, and it is branded as "Rotten" if its score is below 60 percent. Additionally, a movie is deemed "Certified Fresh" if it has a Tomatometer score of 75 percent or higher after having been reviewed by twenty or more critics. Numerous people consult Rotten Tomatoes, apparently on the Condorcetian theory that the average view is likely to be highly reliable.

An alternative method can be found on eBay, which contains an especially admired system for providing feedback on transactions. After a transaction is completed, both the buyer and the seller are given the opportunity to leave comments about the transaction, and to rate the transaction as "positive," "negative," or "neutral." EBay tallies the scores (with a positive being worth +1, a neutral being worth zero, and a negative being worth –1) and prominently places the user's "feedback rating" next to her user ID. For each user, eBay also reveals the percentage of total feedback that is positive.

In addition, eBay allows users to post brief messages explaining their feedback ratings, and if the feedback is neutral or negative, the recipient is allowed to reply to the message. The eBay site allows users to see the feedback that a user has left for others—if, for example, one user appears overeager to leave negative feedback, other users might choose not to do business with that person. One of the valuable features of the eBay feedback mechanism is that both buyers and sellers—even those who use eBay infrequently—almost universally participate in the feedback process. Indeed, eBay goes so far as to send reminder emails to users who have not yet left feedback for a completed transaction.

It would be easy to imagine many uses for mechanisms of this kind. Lior Strahilevitz, for example, has suggested that communities might build on the use of "How am I driving?" bumper stickers by commercial truckers, creating general use of such stickers with the goal of decreasing highway accidents by enlisting many minds.[60] The possibilities seem endless.

I have covered many areas in this chapter, and it will help to offer a summary by way of conclusion.

Even though the price system is not involved, Wikipedia works extraordinarily well, because so many people are both willing and able to cooperate. The wiki form allows anyone to edit, and thus provides an exceptional opportunity to aggregate the information held by many minds. Wikipedia itself offers a series of deliberative forums in which disagreements can be explored. But we can also identify conditions under which wikis will do poorly. If vandals are numerous, if contributors are confused or prone to error, or if people are simply unwilling to devote their labor for free, the success of Wikipedia will not be replicated. Fortunately, the conditions for wikis are often good; hence there are numerous opportunities for using the wiki form to aggregate knowledge.

Of the new methods I have explored here, including prediction markets, open source software may well be the most unambiguous success. A number of factors have made this possible. Many people are willing and able to contribute, sometimes with the prospect of economic reward, sometimes without any such prospect. It is often easy to see whether proposed changes are good ones. For open source projects, filters are put in place to protect against errors. The problems associated with deliberation can be reduced because we are often dealing with eureka-type problems, where deliberation works well. Open source projects typically combine deliberation with access to widely dispersed information and creativity. For this reason, they provide an exciting model, one that might well be adapted to many domains.

It is true that one cannot say, in the abstract, whether open source methods will work better than proprietary ones. For many commodities, internal labor and deliberation, with a direct profit motive, will be best. The success of open source software does, however, give reason to explore the use of the same approach in many other arenas, through a system that includes significant deliberation and numerous contributors.

With respect to the blogosphere, the picture is mixed, notwithstanding Posner's enthuasiastic invocation of Hayek. The immense range of voices unquestionably adds to the stock of perspectives and information in a way that can and does correct social errors. A larger marketplace of ideas is a better marketplace of ideas. On the other hand, the world of blogs is full of many things, including mistakes, confusion, and sheer rage. In many domains, people understand much more because of the existence of blogs. But in some domains, they understand less.

Chapter Six / **Implications and Reforms**

We have seen that there are multiple ways of aggregating information—of taking advantage of the widely dispersed knowledge that individuals have. If groups want to make better decisions, they ought to try to take advantage of that knowledge. Under what circumstances should one or another approach be chosen?

For the prices of commodities, the answer is absurdly easy: Markets are best. It would be extremely foolish to set prices by taking the average judgment of a large group of people. Compared to the choices of statistical groups, deliberation might be better, but it might well be worse. Imagine a set of deliberators deciding on the price of cars or sneakers. Ignorance and self-interest, not to mention group polarization, are likely to produce absurd outcomes. Open source methods provide no sensible way to set prices for commodities. (How could they possibly work?) Many bloggers know a lot, but the blogosphere would be an utterly hopeless place to set prices.

To recapitulate: The advantage of markets lies in the fact that they provide strong incentives for the use and revelation of relevant information, while also allowing bits of knowledge to be incorporated in prices. Markets reflect not only knowledge; they reflect tastes as well. There should be nothing controversial in this claim. It is simply a restatement of Hayek's arguments for markets over socialist-style planning. To be sure, Hayek was too optimistic, and prices can reflect errors, fads, and confusion, sometimes for a long time. But if the question is comparative—What method is best for setting prices?—markets are certainly the best choice.

The same points suggest the potential value of relying on prediction markets whenever institutions and groups want access to highly dispersed information. Suppose that a company is seeking to assess the potential of a particular product. If so, prediction markets, either internal or external, may well be better than the available alternatives. Google has found that internal markets are extremely helpful, and if they work for Google, other companies probably will and should follow. (We can easily foresee a prediction market cascade.) If the question is the likely winner of an Oscar, or the probability of a natural disaster, or the outcome of an election, there is every reason to pay a great deal of attention to prediction markets. I have suggested that in many domains, private and public institutions should consider the use of such markets to supplement deliberative processes. Government agencies, including those involved with national security (such as the Department of Defense and the Central Intelligence Agency), should experiment with internal prediction markets.

To be sure, we do not yet know exactly when prediction markets will work. (Perhaps a prediction market could tell us; shall we bet?) We do know that when people lack information to aggregate, prediction markets are not particularly helpful. But we also know enough to know that in many domains, knowledge is widely dispersed, and such markets hold out a great deal of promise. One of my major suggestions has been that groups and institutions should take advantage of such markets far more than they now do. The Internet makes this extremely easy.

Many people have expressed great enthusiasm for surveys as a means of obtaining dispersed wisdom, and surveys do build on the uncanny accuracy of group averages in predicting heights, weights, and much more. It is tempting to suggest that instead of relying on experts or even markets, institutions should take a large sample and trust the average answer. I have raised serious doubts about this suggestion. It is true that the average answer is likely to be good when most individuals are more likely than not to be right. It follows that when there is reason to trust those who are being surveyed, the group average is likely to be trustworthy as well. Hence leaders, political and corporate, would do well to ask a group of (trusted) advisors about the proper course of action, and to take the average answer unless there is good reason not to do so.

But in many contexts, biases and errors are systematic rather than random; in such contexts, it makes no sense at all to rely on the average answer of large populations. A trivial example: Suppose the question is the color of my dog. If this question were posed to all Americans, it is most doubtful that the plurality answer would be right. (He's a Rhodesian Ridgeback, and his color is red wheaten.) A less trivial example: Suppose the question is the number of human deaths that will be attributable, by 2100, to global warming. Why should we trust the average answer? Where people's answers are worse than random, and where there is a systematic bias, the average answer is not going to be accurate.

As I have emphasized, markets have many advantages over surveys because they create incentives for people to be right and because those who lack information are unlikely to participate. When prediction markets do well, it is because the average contributor is particularly likely to be right; the economic incentive is extremely helpful. But surveys do not have this feature. It is true that if we are seeking access to dispersed information, a group average is probably preferable to the view of a randomly selected person. But there is no *general* reason to trust groups of ordinary people over experts, and there is every reason to favor prediction markets over surveys.

What about deliberation? It is tempting to think that deliberating groups will do better than statistical groups. In such groups, the exchange of perspectives and reasons might ensure that the truth will emerge. But deliberation contains a serious risk: People may not say what they know, and so the information contained in the group as a whole may be neglected or submerged in discussion. Economic incentives reduce this risk; so, too, with the set of norms that underlie open source software and Wikipedia. But we have seen that there is no systematic evidence that deliberating groups will arrive at the truth. On the contrary, it is not even clear that deliberating groups will do better than statistical groups. Sometimes they do, especially on eureka-type problems, where the answer, once announced, appears correct to all. But when the answer is not obviously right, and when individual members tend toward a bad answer, the group is likely to do no better than a statistical group. It might even do worse. The results include many failures in both business and governance.

But my central goal has not been to criticize deliberation as such. The discussion of the newer methods for aggregating dispersed information—prediction markets, wikis, open source software, and blogs—raises an important question: How can deliberating groups counteract the problems I have emphasized? The basic goal should be to increase the likelihood that deliberation will do what it is supposed to do: elicit information, promote creativity, improve decisions. It is possible to draw many lessons from an understanding of alternative ways of obtaining the views of many minds.

We have seen that wikis and open source software work because people are motivated to contribute to the ultimate product. We have also seen that prediction markets do well because they create material incentives to get the right answer. In deliberating groups, by contrast, mistakes often come from informational and reputational pressure. If deliberating groups are to draw on the successes of markets, open source software, and wikis, then the solution is simple: *Groups should take firm steps to increase the likelihood that people will disclose what they know.*

Deliberating groups may not be willing or able to provide economic rewards, as markets do, but they should attempt to create their own incentives for disclosure. Social norms are what make wikis work (recall Wikiquette), and they are crucial here. If people are asked to think critically rather than simply to join the group, and they are told that the group seeks and needs individual contributions, then disclosure is more likely. Consider here a fundamental redefinition of what it means to be a team player. Frequently, a team player is thought to be someone who does not upset the group's consensus. But it would be possible, and a lot better, to understand team players as those who increase the likelihood that the team will be right—if necessary, by disrupting the conventional wisdom.

The point applies to many organizations, including corporate boards. In the United States, the highest-performing companies tend to have "extremely contentious boards that regard dissent as an obligation" and that "have a good fight now and then."[1] On such boards, "even a single dissenter can make a huge difference." Consider, for example, the proposed decision by Medtronic, a large corporation, to acquire Alza, a maker of drug-delivery systems. Medtronic's board was nearly unanimous, but a lone dissenter held out in opposition, urging that this was an area in which Medtronic lacked expertise. The dissenter convinced the board to abandon a proposed acquisition that would almost certainly have proved unprofitable. Another dissenter was able to persuade Medtronic's board to remain in the angioplasty business, a highly profitable decision.[2]

Or consider the account offered by Luther Gulick, a high-level official in the Roosevelt administration during World War II. In 1948, shortly after the Allied victory, Gulick compared the war-making capacities of democracies with those of their fascist adversaries. He noted that the initial evaluation of the United States among the leaders of Germany and Japan was "not flattering." We were, in their view, "incapable of quick or effective national action even in our own defense because under democracy we were divided by our polyglot society and under capitalism deadlocked by our conflicting private interests."[3] Dictatorships could rely on a single leader and an integrated hierarchy, making it easier to develop national unity and enthusiasm, to overcome surprise, and to act vigorously and with dispatch. But these claims about the advantages of totalitarian regimes turned out to be "bogus."

The United States and its allies performed far better than Germany, Italy, and Japan. Gulick linked their superiority directly to "the kind of review and criticism which democracy alone affords." With a totalitarian regime, plans "are hatched in secret by a small group of partially informed men and then enforced through dictatorial authority." Such plans are likely to contain fatal weaknesses. By contrast, a democracy allows wide criticism and debate by many minds, thus avoiding "many a disaster." In a totalitarian system, criticisms and suggestions are neither wanted nor heeded. "Even the leaders tend to believe their own propaganda; they live in cocoons. All of the stream of authority and information is from the top down," so that when change is needed, the high command never learns of that need. But in a democracy, "the public and the press have no hesitation in observing and criticizing the first evidence of failure once a program has been put into operation."[4] In a democracy, information flows within the government, between the lowest and highest ranks, and via public opinion.

Even in a democracy, however, the flow of information does not always work well. I have referred to the failures at the CIA regarding weapons of mass destruction in Iraq, and at NASA involving safety issues for the space shuttles. It would be easy to proliferate examples. But institutional reforms can do a lot to counteract the underlying problems. They can help deliberating groups to operate more like those involved in improving open source software. It is certainly possible to reduce the risk of hidden profiles, cascade effects, and group polarization.

For private and public institutions, the overriding question is how to alter people's incentives in such a way as to increase the likelihood of disclosure. A company might want to ensure that its employees will identify problems with proposed courses of action, even if management is enthusiastic about them. A government might want lower-level officials to point out the risks associated with a plan, perhaps in the area of national security, even if the president himself favors that plan. Many solutions might be imagined.

/ Restructured Incentives /

With open source software, people contribute in part because innovation improves people's reputations. When we silence ourselves in deliberating groups, it is partly because of social norms—because of a sense that our reputation will suffer and that we will be punished, not rewarded, for disclosing information that departs from our group's inclination. Hidden profiles remain hidden in large part for this reason; those who disclose unique information face a risk of disapproval. But groups and institutions can either aggravate or eliminate this effect. If consensus is prized, and known to be prized, then self-silencing will be more likely. But if the group is known to welcome new and competing information, then the reward structure will be fundamentally different, and it will encourage much better outcomes.

Striking evidence for this claim comes from hidden profile experiments that prime people by asking them to engage in a prior task that involved either "getting along" or "critical thinking."[5] Once primed by a task that calls for critical thinking, people are far more likely to disclose what they know, and there is a quite substantial reduction of hidden profiles. (Recall that good team players think critically, and they do not always get along.) For both private and public groups, the general lesson is clear. If the group encourages disclosure of information, even if that information opposes the group's inclination, then self-silencing will be reduced significantly. Deliberation is likely to benefit as a result. Good norms, and a good culture, can go a long way toward reducing the potentially bad effects of social pressures.

/ Rewarding Group Success /

We have seen that people often do not disclose what they know because they receive only a fraction of the benefits of disclosure. But how would groups do if individuals knew that they would be rewarded, not if their own answer was correct, but if the majority of the group was correct?

It might be speculated that in a situation of this kind, hidden profiles, cascades, and group polarization would be reduced dramatically. The reason is that when people are rewarded when their group is right, they are far more likely to reveal to that group what they actually know. In such a situation, incentives are changed so that people internalize the benefits of disclosure. Good leaders are entirely aware of that fact.

Careful experiments show that it is possible to restructure incentives in just this way, and hence to reduce the likelihood of cascades.[6] Cascades are far less likely when each individual knows that she has nothing to gain from a correct *individual* decision and everything to gain from a correct *group* decision. Groups produce much better outcomes when it is in individuals' interest to say exactly what they see or know; the reason is that it is the accurate announcement, from each person, that is most likely to promote an accurate group decision.

An emphasis on the importance of group success should improve decisions in many real-world contexts simply because that emphasis makes it possible to get better access to more minds. Consider the case of whistleblowing, which makes many groups work better. Whistleblowing is often a product not of the whistleblower's narrow self-interest, but of the whistleblower's belief that it is important to take steps to ensure that the organization or group acts properly. Whistleblowers, in short, usually try to promote their group's interest rather than their own. In fact, whistleblowers work a little like participants on Wikipedia or contributors to open source software.

The general lesson is that identification with the group's success is more likely to ensure that people will say what they know. And if group members focus on their own personal prospects, rather than that of the group, the group is more likely to err. Both social norms and material incentives can play crucial roles in establishing the priorities of group members. Wikipedia and open source software benefit from good norms; markets benefit from strong incentives. The trick is to introduce one or the other, or both, into deliberating groups.

/ Of Status and Leadership /

Some people are more likely to silence themselves than others. For example, group members are more likely to speak out if they have high social status or are extremely confident about their own views.[7] I have referred to the complementary finding that members of low-status groups—less educated people, African Americans, sometimes women—carry little influence in deliberating groups.[8] On juries, lower-status members, as measured by their occupation and sex, have been found to be less active and less influential in deliberation.[9] Creative groups would do well to take account of these findings and try to counteract the problems that they reveal.

In prediction markets, low-status people can and do participate; often, they drive predictions in the right direction. In some companies, low-level employees produce predictions that surprise management; we encountered an example at Microsoft. On wikis, status is largely irrelevant; what matters is what you know, not who you are. At least to some extent, the same is true for open source software. Deliberating groups should take steps to ensure that those with information will reveal it.

For example, the risk that unshared information will have insufficient influence is much reduced when that information is held by a leader within a group. Not surprisingly, leaders are entirely willing to share the information they hold. The leader's words usually count, because people listen to what leaders have to say.[10] Consider a revealing experiment: A medical team consisting of a resident physician, an intern, and a third-year medical student was asked to diagnose an illness. The team showed a strong tendency to emphasize unshared items stressed by the resident. In this particular respect, they did not fall prey to the problem of hidden profiles because the resident's information, even though uniquely held, was transferred to all group members.[11] More generally, those experienced in the task at hand are more likely to mention and to repeat unshared information.[12]

One reason for these findings is that those with higher status or competence are less subject to the reputational pressures that lead people to silence themselves.[13] Another reason is that leaders and experts are more likely to think that their own information is accurate and worth disclosing to the group, notwithstanding the fact that the information held by other group members cuts in the other direction.

The simplest lesson is that leaders and high-status members can do groups a great service by indicating their willingness and even desire to hear information that is held by one or a few members and that might otherwise receive little or no attention. Leaders can also refuse to state a firm view at the outset and in that way allow space for more information to emerge. Consider the distinctive practice of President Franklin Delano Roosevelt, who sometimes took the ingenious approach of privately indicating his agreement with multiple advisors whose positions were inconsistent. This approach helped to spur people to develop the best arguments on behalf of their position. When the president was ready to make up his mind, it was only after he had heard sincere and vigorous statements of conflicting positions offered by people who believed, firmly if erroneously, that the president was already on their side.

/ Predeliberation Anonymity, Secret Ballots, and the Delphi Method /

To overcome social influences, people might be asked to state their opinions anonymously, either in advance of deliberation or after deliberation has occurred. The secret ballot can be understood as an effort to insulate people from social pressures and to permit them to say what they believe. Prediction markets work because people invest as they see fit; they do not have to worry that other people will be upset with them. Many institutions should consider more use of the secret ballot simply to elicit more information.

As an ambitious and formal effort to implement this idea, consider the Delphi technique, a process for aggregating the views of group members. The Delphi technique, which can be undertaken via computer or in ordinary space, has several key features. First, it ensures the anonymity of all members through a private statement of views. The purpose of anonymity is precisely to diminish the effects of social pressures, as from dominant or dogmatic individuals, or from a majority." Second, people are given an opportunity to offer feedback on one another's views. Group members are permitted to communicate, sometimes fully but sometimes only their ultimate conclusions. The conclusions, given anonymously, are often provided to others by a facilitator or monitor team, sometimes in the form of a simple summary such as a mean or median value of the group response. Thus, "the feedback comprises the opinions and judgments of all group members and not just the most vocal."[14] Finally, and after the relevant communication, the judgments of group members are elicited and subject to a statistical aggregation.

The Delphi technique provides a sharp contrast with efforts to obtain the judgments of statistical groups and also with interacting groups containing open deliberation. In several contexts, the Delphi technique has produced more accurate results than open discussion.[15] For general almanac questions, the Delphi technique yielded better answers than individual estimates, though open discussion did still better, apparently because it served to correct errors.[16] Note here that the Delphi technique is more successful when group members are provided not only with the mean or median estimate, but also with the reasons given by group members for their views.[17] An account of reasons is most likely to move people in the direction of the correct answer.[18] New technologies can easily be enlisted in the use of the Delphi technique.

Recall the experiment in which people were asked to consider specified heights and weights, and to say whether people with those heights and weights are more likely to be male or female.[19] As we saw, deliberating groups did not do better than statistical groups on that task; often they did worse. But the authors actually tried a third method of aggregating opinions, one close to the Delphi technique. Under that method, people were asked to make private estimates initially, then a period of discussion followed, and then people were asked to make final estimates. These were the most successful groups. A simple approach of "estimate-talk-estimate" radically reduced errors.

A natural alternative to the Delphi technique would be a system in which ultimate judgments are stated anonymously, but only after deliberation. Anonymity, both in advance and in conclusions, would insulate group members from reputational pressure, and to that extent could reduce the problem of self-silencing. Many groups should be experimenting with the Delphi technique and imaginable variations.

/ Devil's Advocates /

If hidden profiles and self-silencing are the source of group failure, then an obvious response is to ask some group members to act as devil's advocates, urging a position that is contrary to the group's inclination. This was a central suggestion of both the Senate committee reporting on intelligence failures in connection with Iraq and of the review board that investigated large blunders at NASA. We have seen that successful leaders, like President Franklin Delano Roosevelt, may try to elicit diverse views by indicating agreement with different (and incompatible) positions. The idea of the devil's advocate is meant to formalize this idea.

Those assuming the role of devil's advocate should not face the social pressure that comes from rejecting the dominant position within the group. After all, they are charged with doing precisely that. And because they are asked to take a contrary position, they are freed from the informational influences that can lead to self-silencing. Hidden profiles are less likely to remain hidden if one or more group members are told to disclose the information they have, even if that information runs contrary to the apparent tendency within the group. In a hidden profile experiment, a devil's advocate should be able to do a lot of good. Note that in the blogosphere, it is tempting to try to make a name for oneself, or at least to have a little fun, by taking a contrarian position. The question is whether deliberating groups can give people an incentive to challenge the emerging or conventional wisdom.

In at least one well-known case, this approach appeared to work. "During the Cuban missile crisis, President Kennedy gave his brother, the Attorney General, the unambiguous mission of playing devil's advocate, with seemingly excellent results in breaking up a premature consensus,"[20] a consensus that might well have led to war.

Research on devil's advocacy in small groups provides suggestive evidence of the effectiveness of devil's advocacy in real-world settings.[21] Many experimenters have found that protection of genuine dissenting views can enhance group performance.[22] But a formal requirement of devil's advocacy enhances group performance far less than does authentic dissent. When an advocate's challenges to a group consensus are insincere, members discount her arguments accordingly. At best, the advocate merely facilitates a more sophisticated inquiry into the problem at hand.[23] Because devil's advocates have no real incentive to sway the group's members to their side, they accomplish their task even if they allow the consensus view to refute their unpopular arguments. Unlike a genuine dissenter, the devil's advocate has little to gain by zealously challenging the dominant view—and as a result tends not to persist in challenging the consensus.[24]

The lesson is that if devil's advocacy is to work, it is because the dissenter actually seems to mean what she is saying. If so, better decisions can be expected.

/ Roles, Experts, and Forewarning /
Imagine a deliberating group consisting of people with specific roles that are appreciated and known by all group members. One person might have medical expertise; another might be a lawyer; a third might know about public relations; a fourth might be a statistician. In such a group, we might speculate that sensible information aggregation would be far more likely simply because each member

knows, in advance, that each of the others has something particular to contribute. Hidden profiles should be less likely to remain hidden if there is a strict division of labor, in which each person is knowledgeable, and known to be knowledgeable, about something in particular.[25]

Several experiments support this hypothesis.[26] In one such experiment, each member of a three-person group was given a good deal of information about one of three murder suspects.[27] In half of these groups, the expertise of each member was publicly identified to everyone before discussion began; in the other half, there was no such public identification of the experts. The bias in favor of shared information was substantially reduced in those groups in which experts were publicly identified as such. The public identification operated as a healthy corrective. But the reduction of the bias was significantly smaller when experts were not identified publicly and when each group member was privately told, by the experimenter, that he or she was an expert on a particular candidate.

Note that prediction markets pretty automatically overcome this bias by creating a financial incentive; the trick is to replicate this happy outcome in deliberating groups. The lesson is clear: If a group wants to obtain the information that its members hold, all group members should be told, before deliberation begins, that different members have different, and relevant, information to contribute. The effect of role assignment in reducing hidden profiles, though not huge, is significant.[28]

/ What Might Be Done /
These findings offer a host of lessons about how deliberating groups might reduce the harmful effects of informational influences and social pressures. The lessons apply to such

diverse groups as corporate boards, government agencies, university faculties, religious institutions, workplaces, juries, and administrative agencies. If information is dispersed within the group, leaders would do well not to state a firm view at the outset; they might well refrain from expressing any opinion at all until other people have said what they think. Following Roosevelt's model, they might indicate sympathy for a wide range of views, encouraging diverse opinions to arise. They might suggest in particular that they welcome information and perspectives that diverge from their own. A degree of impartiality on the part of leaders would go a long way toward encouraging diversity of views. And if reasonable alternatives are not being discussed, group members might be assigned the task of developing and presenting them. Independent subcommittees might be asked to generate new views, possibly views that compete with one another.

Return, for example, to the CIA and NASA examples explored in the introduction. As we have seen, investigators found that the many minds in these agencies had enough information to prevent their large-scale blunders. If internal processes had been properly structured, those blunders would have been far less likely to occur. Suppose that a norm of critical thinking had been firmly encouraged, so that employees would have felt free to challenge assumptions about weapons of mass destruction in Iraq or about the assumed safety of the *Challenger* and *Columbia* flights. Or suppose that both agencies had created an internal system of checks and balances, ensuring careful attention to competing views. If so, relevant information—about the presence of such weapons and about flight safety—would probably have emerged, and been taken seriously, during internal processes.

Of course, time is limited, and prescriptions that are suitable for some organizations will not be suitable for others. In the context of jury deliberations, subcommittees would make little sense; what is required is an initial degree of openness in which jurors explore relevant facts before announcing a conclusion. For government agencies, by contrast, competing subdivisions can help to ensure a range of perspectives. In just this vein, Christopher Edley has suggested that Congress should create, within the Department of Homeland Security, an independent Office on Rights and Liberties, whose specific mission would be to ensure that the effort to protect the nation from terrorist threats does not unduly compromise individual rights.[29] In Edley's account, the office would receive and address public complaints about rights violations; it would also make classified quarterly reports to Congress and the president, along with unclassified reports to the public. The proposal deserves serious consideration as a check on amplification of errors, hidden profiles, and group polarization.[30] There is a serious risk that executive officials will sacrifice liberty in the interest of security. Much help could be provided by a system of the sort that Edley suggests.

An optimistic view of the structure of the Environmental Protection Agency would be that the proliferation of offices with overlapping tasks, including a pro-regulatory Air Office and a more economically oriented Planning Office, ensures a kind of internal system of checks and balances.[31] Under existing law, the independent regulatory agencies, including the Securities and Exchange Commission and the Federal Communications Commission, may not have more than a bare majority of their members from a single political party; both Democrats and Republicans must serve in high positions. This requirement is best understood as an effort to protect against the problems that are likely to result if deliberations are restricted to like-minded people.

Many variations on these themes might be imagined. My goal here has not been to set out an institutional blueprint, but to suggest the general points that deliberating groups should take into account when structuring their processes for aggregating information and points of view. In these ways, the modern successes of prediction markets, wikis, and open source software might be brought directly to bear on some time-honored problems.

/ When Silence Is Golden /

For those who seek to diminish the effects of informational pressure and social influences, a cautionary note remains. We can imagine groups and societies that actually benefit from these effects, and hence from cascades and polarization. Sometimes it is excellent for people to silence themselves. Sometimes their contributions are unhelpful because what they think is untrue.

Suppose that some group members have a terrible idea about how to stabilize the economy, increase corporate earnings, improve a high school, or reduce the threat of terrorism. If so, we should be grateful for informational pressure and social influences because they lead those with bad ideas to defer to others who know much better. As a result of those pressures and that deference, the group's decisions will be improved. If many group members are wrong, it isn't best to elicit their views.

We have seen that polarization might well lead people in the right direction. If people tend to think that communism is bad, it's good for them to end up believing that communism is horrible. If people are prone to favor democracy, it's good if they end up strongly favoring democracy. The question is whether a more extreme version of members' antecedent tendency is correct, and that question must be answered on its merits. Nothing in group polarization shows that those who move are moving toward error.

Or consider a cascade in which the early speakers actually know the truth, and in which those who follow them are ignoring private information that they believe to be true but that would turn out to be wrong or misleading. If so, the followers are not merely rational in disregarding what they know; they are also helping to lead the group in a far better direction because they do not give it bad signals. The most important point here is that if those who start cascades are correct, both individuals and groups are better off as a result.

My emphasis throughout has been on the problems that stem from self-silencing. Good institutions usually need access to many minds, simply for Hayek's reason: Many minds are likely to have a great deal of information. Of course, we should not ignore the possibility that silence is golden. When a few really do know the truth, it is fine for the rest of us to defer to them. But a simple belief, amply vindicated by experience, lies behind democracy and free markets, too. The belief is that on most occasions, the full truth is inaccessible to the few, and hence deference to autocrats and confident planners is a big mistake.

Conclusion / **Realizing Promises**

Is human knowledge a wiki? What is known is certainly a product of countless minds, constantly adding to existing information. Each of us depends on those who came before. Sir Isaac Newton famously captured the point, writing in 1676 to fellow scientist Robert Hooke, "What Descartes did was a good step. You have added much. . . . If I have seen further it is by standing on the shoulders of giants."

Biology, chemistry, physics, economics, psychology, linguistics, history, and many other fields are easily seen as large wikis, in which existing entries, reflecting the stock of knowledge, are "edited" all the time. But this is only a metaphor. No wiki reliably captures any single field, and it is impossible to find a global wiki that contains all of them. And it is easy to find disagreement across human communities about what counts as knowledge within relevant fields. A little example: As a visitor to China in the late 1980s, I was taken by my host to a museum in Beijing, where we came across an exhibit about Genghis Khan. Seeing that name, and without stopping to think, I remarked, "He was a terrible tyrant." My host responded, politely but with conviction, "No, he was a great leader." Trying to recover from my faux pas, I promptly said, by way of excuse, "In school in the United States, we are taught that he was a terrible tyrant." My host replied, also by way of excuse, "In school in China, we are taught that he was a great leader."

Notwithstanding persistent disagreements, new technologies are making it stunningly simple for each of us to obtain dispersed information—and to harness that information, and dispersed creativity as well, for the development of beneficial products and activities. It is child's play not only to find facts, but also to find people's evaluations of countless things, including medicine, food, films, books, cars, law, and history itself. (If you'd like to learn more about Genghis Khan, and about why my Chinese host and I disagreed about him, have a quick look under "Genghis Khan" in Wikipedia.)

It is tempting to think that if many people believe something, there is good reason to assume that they are right. How can many people be wrong? One of my main goals has been to answer that question. People influence one another, and the errors of a few can turn into the errors of the many. Sometimes large groups live in information cocoons. Sometimes diverse people end up occupying echo chambers simply because of social dynamics. Governments no less than educational institutions and businesses fail as a result. I have tried to explain how this is possible.

At the same time, groups and institutions often benefit from widely dispersed knowledge and from the fact that countless people have their own relevant bits of information. For many organizations, and for private and public institutions alike, the key task is to obtain and aggregate the information that people actually hold. We have seen many possible methods. Polls might be taken. People might deliberate. Markets might be used to aggregate preferences and beliefs. Dispersed pieces of information, reflecting dispersed creativity, might be collected through the different methods represented by wikis, open source software, and blogs. Because of the Internet, diverse people, with their own knowledge, are able to participate in the creation of prices, products, services, reports, evaluations, and goods, often to the benefit of all.

Some people are using the Internet to create a kind of Daily Me, in the form of a personalized communications universe limited to congenial points of view. But the more important development is the emergence of a Daily Us, a situation in which people can obtain immediate access to information held by all or at least most, and in which each person can instantly add to that knowledge. To an increasing extent, this form of information aggregation is astonishingly easy. It is transforming businesses, governments, and individual lives.

/ Many Minds, Many Methods /

It is true that on some issues, the average view of large numbers of people is eerily accurate. If most people are more likely to be right than wrong, and if the group is big enough, the majority's view will turn out to be correct. This conclusion follows from the Condorcet Jury Theorem, and it helps explain reliance on aggregated judgments in many contexts, including evaluations of movies, books, cars, and services. We all benefit from such aggregated evaluations, not least because they increase the incentive to improve products. But I have also emphasized the dark side of the Jury Theorem: When most people are more likely to be wrong than right, the likelihood that the majority's position will be wrong approaches 100 percent as the size of the group expands.

It follows that when many or most people's judgments are systematically biased, the average position is wholly unreliable. If everyone in the world were asked to estimate the number of people in the world, there would be no reason to trust the average answer. And if everyone in the world were asked whether global warming is a serious problem, whether a free trade agreement will increase employment, and whether prediction markets produce accurate answers, the answers are not likely to be worth much.

Some of the time, experts' conclusions are far better than populationwide averages. But even when this is so, it might well be better to take the opinion of the average expert, within a group of experts, than to rely on any particular one. The problem—a quite serious one—is that experts might be biased, too. Consider whether foreign policy experts are unerring in their judgments about the United States, France, Israel, North Korea, Iraq, Iran, and Saudi Arabia.

Many groups, both private and public, like to use deliberation, and hence I have focused on that method as a way to aggregate and to filter individual views and opinions. In the abstract, it is tempting to think that deliberation will ensure that groups do at least as well as their best members, or even that they will produce a kind of synergy and learning that should yield excellent judgments. Unfortunately, deliberative bodies are subject to exceedingly serious problems. Much of the time, informational influences and social pressures lead people not to say what they know. As a result, groups tend to propagate, and even to amplify, cognitive errors.

Groups also emphasize information held by all or most at the expense of information held by one or a few; hidden profiles are a result. Deliberating groups often fail to take advantage of the knowledge of a small minority of their members. Moreover, the very process of deliberation can ensure an undue influence from those who are leaders, confident, impressive, or "cognitively central," in the sense that their own information overlaps with that of many group members. Cascade effects are common, potentially spreading errors. Recall the widespread belief that weapons of mass destruction would be found in Iraq. One of the primary effects of deliberation is group polarization, which leads to extremism. Recall the Colorado experiment, where both liberal and conservative groups became more extreme, more uniform in their views, and more sharply divided from one another.

These problems make it possible for deliberating groups to blunder even if the participants behave in accordance with the appealing principles of honesty, equality, and mutual respect. Those who practice deliberation, or celebrate it, have not adequately engaged with existing knowledge, both theoretical and empirical, about how individuals and groups actually behave.

The price system provides a radically different method of aggregating the views of many minds. Prices reflect the beliefs and tastes of numerous people. For reasons traced by Hayek, the price system can work amazingly well as an aggregative mechanism. Stock prices also reflect an aggregation of views, and here there is an intense debate about the reliability of the aggregation. Much of the time, the stock market does indeed do well. Unfortunately, the same problems that infect deliberating groups can infect markets, with informational cascades, for example, leading people to serious errors. Fads and fashions affect investments as well as deliberation.

But my particular focus has been on prediction markets, which are at once newer and simpler. As we have seen, prediction markets often produce extremely good answers. Such markets tend to correct rather than to amplify individual errors, above all because they allow shrewd investors to take advantage of the mistakes made by others. Because prediction markets provide economic rewards for correct answers, they align people's incentives in a way that promotes disclosure. As a result, they are often more accurate than the judgments of deliberating groups. Highly successful companies, including Google and Microsoft, are using them. They should be, and will be, exploited far more often by the private and public sectors.

Wikis and open source software aggregate information in still different ways. They cannot use the price signal, but they do generate a product. Some contributors lack any kind of economic incentive, but they usually behave in good faith. When the system is working well, wikis and open source products aggregate dispersed bits of knowledge and creativity, yielding dramatically more than any single mind could have produced on its own. One of the advantages of wikis is their extraordinary flexibility; they, too, deserve far more use by private companies and government. I have devoted special attention to Wikipedia, but there are many other successful wikis, and it is easy to imagine little wikis used by companies and organizations of many different kinds.

Wikipedia has no system for screening, and hence its success could not easily have been predicted. It works because the vast majority of people are operating with knowledge and in good faith. Of course, wikis could not do so well if participants were confused, incompetent, mischievous, biased, or destructive. But because so many human beings want to be helpful, and are able to do so, we should expect many new uses of wikis, and intriguing variations as well.

Open source software works in part because it combines numerous contributors with a process of formal screening that reduces the risk of major blunders. Many contributors are willing to make improvements even without a financial incentive. Much of the excitement of open source software stems from the fact that its success may well be generalizable, extending beyond software to biotechnology, medicine, law, and many other domains. There is no question that open source products are going to do a great deal of good.

Blogs present still different issues. In Hayekian fashion, they can ensure that widely dispersed information is available to those who care to read them. On important occasions, the blogosphere has provided a valuable mechanism not only for mutual correction, but also for correction of more traditional information sources, including the mass media. But blogs are no panacea in the political domain or anywhere else. By their very nature, blogs create the same risks that always accompany deliberation: amplification of errors, cascade effects, hidden profiles, and group polarization. Every day, group polarization occurs on the blogosphere, with like-minded people driving one another to unjustifed extremes, including unjustified extremes of anger and outrage.

I have attempted to draw some general lessons for improving deliberation in the private and public spheres. At the very least, it should be possible to structure deliberation so as to increase the likelihood that valuable information will emerge. A strong norm in favor of critical thinking can reduce some of the most damaging pressures, and hence ensure that people will hear from many minds rather than a few. To encourage a wide range of views, leaders should be cautious about expressing their own views at the outset. They should encourage reasons, rather than conclusions, before the views of group members start to harden. Institutions might allow for anonymity and private polling before deliberation. They might create strong incentives, economic and otherwise, to encourage people to say what they know.

/ Opting for Optimism /

It is tempting to take one of two positions on the topic of this book. The pessimistic view emphasizes mob psychology, groupthink, and the risk that people will lead one another astray, especially if they are like-minded and interacting with one another. Here we can find the fear of information cocoons, echo chambers, and the Daily Me, in which people "customize" their communications universes. Here, too, we can find not only the sources of social hysteria and panics, not based on anything like objective fact, but also the roots of "political correctness" in all its forms, including university campuses, wildly overoptimistic businesses, and the highest reaches of government. We can also identify some of the sources of herd behavior and the most destructive political movements, including Nazism, communism, and terrorism. When groups, localities, and even nations are unjustifiably angry or fearful or fall prey to mass hatred, hidden profiles, cascades, and group polarization are almost always involved.

The optimistic view, rooted in Condorcet and Hayek, stresses the widely dispersed nature of information and the possibility that aggregations of information will prove uncannily accurate. Here we can find the foundations of respect for economic markets and even for traditions, which seem to reflect the views of numerous people across time. In a way, respect for democracy itself stems from the belief that so long as people do not cocoon themselves, large numbers of citizens are not likely to be wrong. The two cornerstones of free societies—markets and democracy—rest on the belief that many minds can be trusted.

We can now see that both positions are much too simple. Mob psychology and groupthink are pervasive, and they are captured in the amplification of errors, hidden profiles, bad cascades, and group polarization. Unfortunately, the Internet makes these easier every day. Healthy aggregation of information is certainly possible. Fortunately, the Internet makes it easier every day.

I have tried to identify the circumstances in which the pessimistic and optimistic visions are most likely to materialize. I have also attempted to show how groups and institutions, both private and public, might increase the likelihood that the optimistic vision will come to fruition. Far more than ever before, humanity has promising methods for seeking out widely dispersed information and creativity and for aggregating these into uncannily productive wholes. The ultimate value of the new methods depends, of course, on how we use them. But if we are going to bet, it makes sense to bet on optimism.

Appendix / **Prediction Markets**

Prediction markets are growing at an explosive rate. For a sense of the variety of what is available, here is a partial list:

- Austrian Political Stock Markets/Austrian Electronic Markets at http://zwickl.ibab.tuwien.ac.at/apsm (predicting outcomes of Austrian elections).
- Celebdaq at www.bbc.co.uk/celebdaq (British market that values celebrities; investors use virtual money to trade shares in celebrities, with amounts paid on the basis of the level of press coverage).
- Economic Derivatives at http://www.economicderiva tives.com (online markets for economic derivatives involving events such as employment statistics, inflation, economic growth, and retail sales).
- Election Stock Market at http://wsm.ubc.ca (allowing real money for bids on outcomes of Canadian elections).
- Foresight Exchange at http://www.ideosphere.com/fx/ (entertainment site allowing users to bet on the likely outcome of future events using "funny money").
- Hollywood Stock Exchange at http://www.hsx.com (allowing users to use virtual money to bet on box office success of actors and movies).
- Influenza Prediction Market at http://iemweb.biz.uiowa. edu/OUTBREAK/flu_quotes.html (market to predict weekly influenza activity; run by Iowa Electronic Markets, by invitation only; virtual money is used but it can be converted into valuable prizes).

- Innovation Futures at www.innovationfutures.com/bk/index_html (permitting use of virtual money to trade contracts involving financial trends and prospects of new technologies; prizes are available to successful investors in the form of merchandise).
- InTrade at http://www.intrade.com (allowing investment of real money to predict numerous events, including politics and sports).
- Iowa Electronic Markets at http://www.biz.uiowa.edu/iem/ (market in which contract payoffs depend on economic and political events).
- Long Bets–Accountable Predictions at http://www.longbets.org (allowing people to predict whether important social or scientific events will happen; $50 bets are allowed; the money is paid to the charity identified by winners).
- News Futures at http://us.newsfutures.com/home/home.html (provider of prediction markets that deliver forecasts on issues for corporations and others).
- Political Stock Exchange at http://www.PoliticalStockExchange.com (allowing participants to use virtual money to purchase shares in political events and politicians).
- Probability Sports at http://www.probabilitysports.com (online sports betting site).
- Tech Buzz Market at http://buzz.research.yahoo.com/bk/index.html (using play money to predict success of new technologies).
- Tradesports at http://www.tradesports.com (online trading exchange focused on the outcome of sporting and other events).
- Wahlstreet at http://www.wahlstreet.de (German political futures market).

- Washington Stock Exchange at http://www.washington sx.com/ (virtual stock market based on future outcomes of U.S. political elections and events).

Notes /

Introduction /

1. "Plant Biotech Goes Open Source," Feb. 10, 2005, http://news.bbc.co.uk/1/hi/sci/tech/4248155.stm.

2. Jamais Carcio, "Open Source Biotech Makes Its Mark," Feb. 10, 2005, http://www.worldchanging.com/archives/002082.html.

3. See "Putting Crowd Wisdom to Work," Sept. 21. 2005, http://googleblog.blogspot.com/2005/09/putting-crowd-wisdom-to-work.html.

4. Nicholas Negroponte, *Being Digital* (New York: Vintage, 1995), 153. In Cass R. Sunstein, *Republic.com* (Princeton, NJ: Princeton University Press, 2001), I extend and explore this possibility.

5. Jürgen Habermas, *Between Facts and Norms: Contributions to a Discourse Theory of Law and Democracy*, trans. William Rehg (Cambridge, MA: MIT Press, 1998) (elaborating deliberative conception of democracy). For other accounts, see generally Jon Elster, ed., *Deliberative Democracy* (New York: Cambridge University Press, 1998) (collecting diverse treatments of deliberative democracy); Amy Gutmann and Dennis Thompson, *Democracy and Disagreement* (Cambridge, MA: Belknap Press, 1996) (defending deliberative democracy and discussing its preconditions). On the role of deliberative democracy in the American framing, see Joseph M. Bessette, *The Mild Voice of Reason* (Chicago: University of Chicago Press, 1994), 6–39.

6. Carl Schmitt, *Crisis of Parliamentary Democracy*, trans. Ellen Kennedy (Cambridge, MA: MIT Press, 1985), 35.

7. For a brief and clear statement of the preconditions for deliberation, see Jürgen Habermas, "Between Facts and Norms: An Author's Reflections," *Denver University Law Review* 76

(1999): 940–41. For an overlapping view emphasizing moral requirements imposed on participants by the deliberative ideal, see Gutmann and Thompson, *Democracy and Disagreement*, 39–51.

8. James S. Fishkin, *The Voice of the People: Public Opinion and Democracy* (New Haven: Yale University Press, 1995), 162–76.

9. Bruce Ackerman and James S. Fishkin, *Deliberation Day* (New Haven: Yale University Press, 2004), 3–16.

10. See Robert J. MacCoun, "Comparing Micro and Macro Rationality," in *Judgments, Decisions, and Public Policy*, ed. Rajeev Gowda and Jeffrey C. Fox (Cambridge, UK: Cambridge University Press, 2002), 121–26; Daniel Gigone and Reid Hastie, "Proper Analysis of the Accuracy of Group Judgment," *Psychological Bulletin* 121 (1997): 161–62; Garold Stasser and William Titus, "Hidden Profiles: A Brief History," *Psychological Inquiry* 14 (2003): 308–9.

11. Irving L. Janis, *Groupthink*, 2d ed., rev. (Boston: Houghton Mifflin, 1982), 7–9.

12. Senate Select Committee on Intelligence, Report of the 108th Congress, *U.S. Intelligence Community's Prewar Intelligence Assessments on Iraq: Conclusions*, 4–7 (full version, S. Rep. No. 108–301, 2004), available at http://intelligence.senate.gov.

13. Ibid., 4.

14. 1 Columbia Accident Investigation Board, NASA, *The Columbia Accident Investigation Board Report*, 2003, 97–204, available at http://www.nasa.gov/columbia/home/CAIB_Vol1.html.

15. Ibid., 12, 102 (internal citation omitted), 183.

16. See Cass R. Sunstein, David Schkade, and Lisa Michelle Ellman, "Ideological Voting on Federal Courts of Appeals: A Preliminary Investigation," *Virginia Law Review* 90 (2004): 304–6, 314 (showing effects of panel composition on judicial behavior); Cass R. Sunstein et al., *Are Judges Political?: An Empirical Analysis of the Federal Judiciary* (Washington, DC: Brookings, 2006).

17. Eric Raymond, *The Cathedral and the Bazaar*, 2d ed. (Sebastopol, CA: O'Reilly, 2001), 30.

18. These often are described as the judgments of "statisticized groups." See Irving Lorge et al., "A Survey of Studies Contrasting the Quality of Group Performance and Individual Performance, 1920–1957," *Psychological Bulletin* 55 (1958): 344.

19. See Habermas, "Between Facts and Norms: An Author's Reflections," 940.

20. Friedrich Hayek, *Law, Legislation, and Liberty*, vol. 1: *Rules and Order* (Chicago: University of Chicago Press, 1973), 13.

21. See Russell Hardin, "The Crippled Epistemology of Extremism," in *Political Rationality and Extremism*, ed. Albert Breton et al. (Cambridge, UK: Cambridge University Press, 2002), 3, 16.

Chapter 1 /

1. See James Surowiecki, *The Wisdom of Crowds: Why the Many Are Smarter Than the Few and How Collective Wisdom Shapes Business, Economies, Societies, and Nations* (New York: Doubleday, 2004).

2. John Zajc, "This Week in SABR" (Society for American Baseball Research, Cleveland, Ohio), Oct. 9, 2004 (Results of playoff prediction survey), available at http://www.sabr.org/ sabr.cfm?a=cms,c,1123,3,212.

3. The story is told in "Kasparov Against the World," http:// en.wikipedia.org/wiki/Kasparov_versus_The_World.

4. See Cass R. Sunstein et al., "Assessing Punitive Damages," *Yale Law Journal* 107 (1998): 2095–99 (showing that small groups often reflect judgments of community as whole, at least when their judgments are made on a bounded scale).

5. See Sergey Brin and Lawrence Page, "The Anatomy of a Large-Scale Hypertextual Web Search Engine," *Computer Networks & ISDN System* 30 (1998): 107–10, available at http://dbpubs .stanford.edu:8090/pub/1998–8.

6. Lorge et al., "A Survey of Studies Contrasting the Quality of Group Performance and Individual Performance, 1920–1957," 344.

7. See Surowiecki, *The Wisdom of Crowds*, 5 (discussing jar experiment).

8. Richard S. Bruce, "Group Judgments in the Field of Lifted Weights and Visual Discrimination," *Journal of Psychology* 1 (1936): 117–21.

9. Surowiecki, *The Wisdom of Crowds*, xi–xiii.

10. Some affirmative evidence can be found in J. Scott Armstrong, "Combining Forecasts," in *Principles of Forecasting*, ed. J. Scott Armstrong (Boston: Kluwer Academic, 2001), 419–20, 427, 433–35.

11. See William P. Bottom et al., "Propagation of Individual Bias through Group Judgment: Error in the Treatment of Asymmetrically Informative Signals," *Journal of Risk and Uncertainty* 25 (2002): 152–54.

12. For the arithmetic: Suppose that a group has N voters, and that they are choosing between two alternatives. Each voter has the same probability, p, of being right, with p being somewhere between 50 percent and 100 percent. Assume, too, that each group member has the same probability of making an accurate decision, and that each member's judgment is statistically independent. The probability, P/n, that the group will reach the right decision by majority rule is captured in this way:
$$P_{n=} \sum_{h=(n+1)/2}^{n} \left[n!/h!(n-h)! \right] p^h (1-p)^{n-h}$$
I draw here on Dennis C. Mueller, *Public Choice III* (Cambridge, UK: Cambridge University Press, 2003), 129; Robert E. Goodin, *Reflective Democracy* (Oxford: Oxford University Press, 2005), 95–96. Thanks to David Weisbach for help.

13. See Zagat Survey Web site, http://www.zagat.com/about/about.aspx.

14. See Goodin, *Reflective Democracy*, 91–108.

15. For important qualifications, see the papers by David M. Estlund and Jeremy Waldron in "Democratic Theory and the Public Interest: Condorcet and Rousseau Revisited," *American Political Science Review* 83 (1989). I draw on these qualifications below.

16. Bernard Grofman and Scott Feld, "Rousseau's General Will: A Condorcetian Perspective," *American Political Science Review* 82 (1988): 567.

17. See Bottom et al., "Propagation of Individual Bias through Group Judgment," 153.

18. Ibid.

19. See David Estlund, *Democratic Authority: A Philosophical Framework* (Princeton, NJ: Princeton University Press, forthcoming): "The mathematical result is beyond dispute, but it only applies under certain conditions. One is that enough of the votes must be statistically independent. This is often misunderstood. On the overly pessimistic side, many have said that this cannot be met since there will always be lots of influence one way or another. Few will be independent of one another. What the theorem requires, though, is not causal independence but statistical independence."

20. Condorcet, *Selected Writings*, ed. Keith Michael Baker (Indianapolis: Bobbs-Merrill, 1976), 62. This point is emphasized in Waldron, "Democratic Theory and the Public Interest," and in Estlund, *Democratic Authority*.

21. See Joseph Henrich et al., "Group Report: What Is the Role of Culture in Bounded Rationality?," in *Bounded Rationality: The Adaptive Toolbox*, ed. Gerd Gigerenzer and Reinhard Selten (Cambridge, MA: MIT Press, 2001), 353–54, for an entertaining outline in connection with food choice decisions.

22. Edward Glaeser, "Psychology and Paternalism," *University of Chicago Law Review* (2001): 133.

23. On some of the technical complexities, see Christian List and Robert E. Goodin, "Epistemic Democracy: Generalizing the Condorcet Jury Theorem," *Journal of Political Philosophy* 9 (2001): 283–88, 295–97.

24. Ibid.

25. See Surowiecki, *The Wisdom of Crowds*, 3–4.

26. Condorcet, *Selected Writings*, 156–57.

27. Even self-evidently arbitrary anchors have significant effects on people's judgments. See Gretchen Chapman and Eric Johnson, "Incorporating the Irrelevant: Anchors in Judgments of Belief and Value," in *Heuristics and Biases: The Psychology of Intuitive*

Judgment, ed. Thomas Gilovich et al. (New York: Cambridge University Press, 2002), 120.

28. Lorge et al., "A Survey of Studies Contrasting the Quality of Group Performance and Individual Performance, 1920–1957," 346.

29. See Reid Hastie et al., "Do Plaintiffs' Requests and Plaintiffs' Identities Matter?," in *Punitive Damages: How Juries Decide,* ed. Cass R. Sunstein et al. (Chicago: University of Chicago Press, 2002), 62, 73–74. See generally Chapman and Johnson, "Incorporating the Irrelevant."

30. Chris Guthrie et al., "Inside the Judicial Mind," *Cornell Law Review* 86 (2001): 790–91 (showing effect of anchors on judicial judgments in experimental contexts).

31. See Norbert L. Kerr et al., "Bias in Judgment: Comparing Individuals and Groups," *Psychological Review* 103 (1996): 689, 691–93 (noting studies showing that anchors affect groups as well as individuals).

32. Condorcet, *Selected Writings,* 49.

33. Ibid., 61.

34. For a classic example, see Bruce Ackerman and William Hassler, *Clean Coal/Dirty Air* (New Haven: Yale University Press, 1983).

35. See Armstrong, "Combining Forecasts," 419–20. For many factual questions, of course, a little research would be sufficient to identify the correct answers. But for some factual issues, even significant research is inconclusive, and it is best to consult experts.

36. Ibid., 428.

37. Ibid., 428, 430–31.

38. Ibid., 433.

39. See Alfred Cuzán et al., "Combining Methods to Forecast the 2004 Presidential Election: The Pollyvote" (unpublished manuscript, Jan. 6, 2005), 12, available at http://www.politi calforecasting.com.

40. Political Forecasting, "Polly's Page," at www.politicalfore casting.com (last updated Jan. 5, 2005).

41. I am grateful to Robert MacCoun for this point.

42. See Bjørn Lomborg ed., *Global Crises, Global Solutions* (Cambridge, UK: Cambridge University Press, 2004), 1–9.

43. In the context of the Copenhagen Consensus, the assessment of the central question—"the best ways of advancing global welfare"—involved normative judgments as well as factual ones. For example, the experts ranked control of malaria above improving infant and child nutrition (see ibid., 606), but this ranking involves contentious judgments of value as well as empirical claims. The simplest way to test the aggregation of expert judgments is through use of predictive questions on which unambiguous evidence is available.

Chapter 2 /

1. See Reid Hastie, David Schkade, and Cass R. Sunstein, "What Really Happened on Deliberation Day?" (University of Chicago Law School, unpublished manuscript, 2006).

2. I draw here on Janis, *Groupthink*, 14–47.

3. Ibid., 16.

4. Ted Sorensen, *Kennedy* (New York: HarperCollins, 1966), 343.

5. Arthur Schlesinger Jr., *A Thousand Days* (New York: Mariner Books, 1965), 258–59.

6. See David Schkade et al., "Deliberating about Dollars: The Severity Shift," *Columbia Law Review* 100 (2000): 101.

7. Aristotle, *Politics*, trans. E. Barker (London: Oxford University Press, 1972), 123.

8. John Rawls, *A Theory of Justice* (Cambridge, MA: Belknap Press, 1971), 358–59.

9. See James Madison, *The Record of the Federal Convention of 1787*, ed. Max Ferrand (New Haven: Yale University Press, 1911).

10. Herbert Storing, ed., *The Complete Anti-Federalist*, vol. 2 (Chicago: University of Chicago Press, 1981), 269.

11. See *The Federalist* No. 70 (Alexander Hamilton), ed. Clinton Rossiter (New York: New American Library, 1961), 426–28.

12. Joseph Gale, ed., *Annals of Congress*, vol. 1 (New York, 1789), 733–45.

13. See David J. Cooper and John H. Kagel, "Are Two Heads Better Than One? Team versus Individual Play in Signalling Games," *American Economic Review* 95 (2005): 477; Gigone and Hastie, "Proper Analysis," 143–53 (offering some examples of group success, while showing that such success is not typical).

14. Chip Heath and Richard Gonzales, "Interaction with Others Increases Decision Confidence but Not Decision Quality: Evidence against Information Collection Views of Interactive Decision Making," *Organizational Behavior and Human Decision Processes* 61 (1997): 305–26.

15. See Rupert Brown, *Group Processes*, 2d ed. (Oxford: Blackwell, 2000), 176: "The groups were also more confident about the correctness of their answers, and this was true even when they got the answers wrong!"

16. See Robert S. Baron et al., "Social Corroboration and Opinion Extremity," *Journal of Experimental Social Psychology* 32 (1996): 538 (discussing effects of corroboration in increasing extremism).

17. See Brown, *Group Processes*, 206–7 (showing reduction in variance).

18. Ibid.

19. Ibid., 173–93 (describing complex results about group performance); Gigone and Hastie, "Proper Analysis," 149, 153 (summarizing studies as finding group judgments to be approximately equal to accuracy of mean judgments of their members, and less accurate than judgments of their most accurate member); Kerr et al., "Bias in Judgment," 713 (finding, after canvassing of empirical literature, "no simple empirical answer" to question of whether individuals or groups are more likely to make biased judgments, and contending that a theoretical analysis helps to identify when groups will be more or less biased than individuals).

20. See Kerr et al., "Bias in Judgment."

21. David H. Gustafson et al., "A Comparative Study of Differences in Subjective Likelihood Estimates Made by Individuals,

Interacting Groups, Delphi Groups, and Nominal Groups," *Organizational Behavior and Human Performance* 9 (1973): 280.

22. See Gigone and Hastie, "Proper Analysis," 153 (summarizing findings that groups do not perform as well as best members); Reid Hastie, "Review Essay: Experimental Evidence of Group Accuracy," in *Information Pooling and Group Decision Making*, ed. Bernard Grofman and Guillermo Owen (Greenwich, CT: JAI Press, 1983), 133–46. To the same effect, see Garold Stasser and Beth Dietz-Uhler, "Collective Choice, Judgment, and Problem Solving," in *Blackwell Handbook of Group Psychology: Group Processes*, ed. Michael A. Hogg and R. Scott Tindale (Oxford: Blackwell, 2001), 49–50 (collecting findings).

23. Hillel J. Einhorn et al., "Quality of Group Judgment," *Psychological Bulletin* 84 (1977): 168.

24. See Hastie, "Review Essay," 133–46 (showing that groups do not usually perform as well as their most accurate individual member).

25. See ibid., 133.

26. See Harold E. Burtt, "Sex Differences in the Effect of Discussion," *Journal of Experimental Psychology* 3 (1920): 390–95.

27. See Hastie, "Review Essay," 147.

28. See ibid., 134–38.

29. See Brown, *Group Processes*, 176.

30. Ibid. (emphasis in original).

31. See Stasser and Dietz-Uhler, "Collective Choice, Judgment, and Problem Solving," 35.

32. Ibid., 40.

33. See Gigone and Hastie, "Proper Analysis," 165.

34. See Norbert L. Kerr and Ernest S. Park, "Group Performance in Collaborative and Social Dilemma Tasks: Progress and Prospects," in Hogg and Tindale, *Group Processes*, 107, 110.

35. See Hastie, "Review Essay," 148.

36. Ibid.

37. See Cooper and Kagel, "Are Two Heads Better Than One?"

38. Alan S. Blinder and John Morgan, *Are Two Heads Better Than One? An Experimental Analysis of Group vs. Individual*

Decisionmaking, National Bureau of Economic Research, Working Paper No. 7909 (2000), 6, 15, 46–47.

39. Ibid., 46.

40. See Garold Stasser and Dennis Stewart, "Discovery of Hidden Profiles by Decision-Making Groups: Solving a Problem versus Making a Judgment," *Journal of Personality and Social Psychology* 63 (1992): 432–33.

41. Ibid., 428.

42. See MacCoun, "Comparing Micro and Macro Rationality," 120 (showing that groups will not arrive at accurate answer unless that answer begins with significant support).

43. Ibid., 120.

44. See ibid.

45. See ibid., 124 (showing that individual biases are often amplified, not diminished, by group interaction).

46. Robert L. Thorndike, "The Effect of Discussion upon the Correctness of Group Decisions, When the Factor of Majority Influence Is Allowed For," *Journal of Social Psychology* 9 (1938): 348–61 (exploring effects of both correctness and majority pressure on group judgments).

47. See Joel Cooper et al., "Attitudes, Norms, and Social Groups," in Hogg and Tindale, *Group Processes*, 259, 260–62.

48. Armstrong, "Combining Forecasts," 433.

49. See the overview in Solomon Asch, "Opinions and Social Pressure," in *Readings about the Social Animal*, ed. Elliott Aronson (New York: W. H. Freeman, 1995), 13.

50. See David Krech et al., *Individual in Society* (New York: McGraw-Hill, 1962), 514 (showing individual susceptibility to majority views).

51. See Brooke Harrington, *Pop Finance: Investment Clubs and the New Ownership Society* (Princeton, NJ: Princeton University Press, forthcoming).

52. See José M. Marques et al., "Social Categorization, Social Identification, and Rejection of Deviant Group Members," in Hogg and Tindale, *Group Processes*, 400, 403.

53. See Glenn C. Loury, *Self-Censorship in Public Discourse: A*

Theory of "Political Correctness" and Related Phenomena, Boston University, Ruth Pollak Working Paper Series on Economics (1993), 3.

54. See Caryn Christensen and Ann S. Abbott, "Team Medical Decision Making," in *Decision Making in Health Care*, ed. Gretchen B. Chapman and Frank A. Sonnenberg (Cambridge, UK: Cambridge University Press, 2000), 272–76 (discussing effects of status on exchange of information in group interactions).

55. See Sunstein, Schkade, and Ellman, "Ideological Voting on Federal Courts of Appeals," 314 (showing effects of panel composition on judicial decisions).

56. See Bibb Latané and Martin J. Bourgeois, "Dynamic Social Impact and the Consolidation, Clustering, Correlation, and Continuing Diversity of Culture," in Hogg and Tindale, *Group Processes*, 235, 237–51.

57. Ibid., 243–46.

58. Habermas, *Between Facts and Norms*, 940.

59. Jürgen Habermas, "What Is Universal Pragmatics?," in *Communication and the Evolution of Society*, trans. Thomas McCarthy (Boston: Beacon Press, 1979), 2–4, 32 (discussing preconditions for communication).

60. See Gutmann and Thompson, *Democracy and Disagreement*, 7–8 (outlining foundations of deliberative democracy).

Chapter 3 /

1. For an overview, see generally Thomas Gilovich et al., eds., *Heuristics and Biases: The Psychology of Intuitive Judgment* (Cambridge, UK: Cambridge University Press, 2002). See also Cass R. Sunstein, ed., *Behavioral Law and Economics* (Cambridge, UK: Cambridge University Press, 2000).

2. See Amos Tversky and Daniel Kahneman, "Availability: A Heuristic for Judging Frequency and Probability," *Cognitive Psychology* 5 (1973): 208 (discussing availability heuristic).

3. Paul Slovic, *The Perception of Risk* (London: Earthscan Publications, 2000), 37–48.

4. Ibid., 40.

5. See Donald A. Redelmeier et al., "Understanding Patients' Decisions: Cognitive and Emotional Perspectives," *Journal of the American Medical Association* 270 (1993): 73 (discussing framing effects in medical context).

6. Amos Tversky and Daniel Kahneman, "Extensional versus Intuitive Reasoning: The Conjunction Fallacy in Probability Judgment," in Gilovich et al., *Heuristics and Biases*, 19, 22–25 (discussing representativeness).

7. See Amos Tversky and Daniel Kahneman, "Judgment under Uncertainty: Heuristics and Biases," in *Judgment under Uncertainty: Heuristics and Biases*, ed. Daniel Kahneman, Paul Slovic, and Amos Tversky (Cambridge, UK: Cambridge University Press, 1982), 11–12; Barbara Mellers et al., "Do Frequency Representations Eliminate Conjunction Effects?," *Psychological Science Journal* 12 (2001).

8. See Stasser and Dietz-Uhler, "Collective Choice, Judgment, and Problem Solving," 49–50. Note that when the bias is not widely shared, it may be corrected through deliberation. See ibid.

9. MacCoun, "Comparing Micro and Macro Rationality," 121–26 (showing amplification of jury bias).

10. Mark F. Stasson et al., "Group Consensus Approaches on Cognitive Bias Tasks: A Social Decision Scheme Approach," *Japanese Psychological Research Journal* 30 (1988): 74–75.

11. See Kerr et al., "Bias in Judgment," 693, 711–12.

12. See ibid., 692, Table 1 (noting study that found groups generally more confident than individuals); Janet A. Sniezek and Rebecca A. Henry, "Accuracy and Confidence in Group Judgment," *Organizational Behavior and Human Decision Processes* 42 (1989): 24–27.

13. See Kerr et al., "Bias in Judgment," 691.

14. Ibid., 692 (citing studies).

15. Ibid.

16. Stasser and Dietz-Uhler, "Collective Choice, Judgment, and Problem Solving," 48.

17. Personal communication with Reid Hastie, University of Chicago Business School (July 24, 2004), who has conducted experiments on this issue for many years.

18. See generally Dagmar Stahlberg et al., "We Knew It All Along: Hindsight Bias in Groups," *Organizational Behavior and Human Decision Processes* 63 (1995): 46.

19. MacCoun, "Comparing Micro and Macro Rationality," 124 (emphasis omitted).

20. See Stasser and Titus, "Hidden Profiles," 304, 306–13 (discussing hidden profile experiments).

21. Daniel Gigone and Reid Hastie, "The Common Knowledge Effect: Information Sharing and Group Judgments," *Journal of Personality and Social Psychology* 65 (1993): 971–73 (explaining hidden profiles by reference to common knowledge effect).

22. See Garold Stasser and William Titus, "Pooling of Unshared Information in Group Decision Making: Biased Information Sampling During Discussion," *Journal of Personality and Social Psychology* 48 (1985): 1471–72.

23. Ibid., 1476.

24. Stasser and Titus, "Hidden Profiles," 305.

25. See Gigone and Hastie, "Common Knowledge Effect," 959 (describing experiment showing common knowledge effect in groups of three).

26. Ibid., 960.

27. Ibid., 973.

28. Ibid.

29. Susanne Abele et al., "Information and Cognitive Centrality," May 2005, available at www.erim.eur.nl.

30. See T. Kameda et al., "Centrality in Sociocognitive Networks and Social Influence: An Illustration in a Group Decision-Making Context," *Journal of Personality and Social Psychology* 73 (1997): 296.

31. See Garold Stasser et al., "Information Sampling in Structured and Unstructured Discussions of Three- and Six-Person Groups," *Journal of Personality and Social Psychology* 57 (1989): 72–73.

32. Ibid., 78.
33. See Stasser and Titus, "Hidden Profiles," 306–7.
34. See Gigone and Hastie, "Common Knowledge Effect,"960.
35. Stasser and Titus, "Hidden Profiles," 308.
36. Ibid.
37. Stasser and Titus, "Hidden Profiles," supra note, 308.
38. Cecilia L. Ridgeway, "Social Status and Group Structure," in Hogg and Tindale, *Group Processes*, 352, 354 (collecting studies).
39. See Gwen M. Wittenbaum et al., "Mutual Enhancement: Toward an Understanding of the Collective Preference for Shared Information," *Journal of Personality and Social Psychology* 77 (1999): 967–78.
40. Stasser and Titus, "Hidden Profiles," 311.
41. I draw here on David Hirshleifer, "The Blind Leading the Blind: Social Influence, Fads, and Informational Cascades," in *The New Economics of Human Behavior*, ed. Mariano Tommasi and Kathryn Ierulli (Cambridge, UK: Cambridge University Press, 1995), 193–95, and on the discussion in Cass R. Sunstein, *Why Societies Need Dissent* (Cambridge, MA: Harvard University Press, 2003), 55–73.
42. Hirshleifer, "The Blind Leading the Blind," 204.
43. John F. Burnham, "Medical Practice a la Mode: How Medical Fashions Determine Medical Care," *New England Journal of Medicine* 317 (1987): 1201.
44. See Sushil Bikhchandani et al., "Learning from the Behavior of Others: Conformity, Fads, and Informational Cascades," *Journal of Economic Perspectives Journal* 12 (1998): 167.
45. See Fabio Lorenzi-Cioldi and Alain Clémence, "Group Processes and the Construction of Social Representations," in Hogg and Tindale, *Group Processes*, 311, 315–17.
46. See Brown, *Group Processes*, 202–26.
47. See ibid., 204.
48. Ibid., 223–24.
49. See John C. Turner, *Rediscovering the Social Group: A Self-Categorization Theory* (New York: Blackwell, 1987), 152–53.
50. Ibid.

51. See Brown, *Group Processes*, 222–24.

52. See Sunstein, Schkade, and Ellman, "Ideological Voting on Federal Courts of Appeals," 305 (showing group polarization within court of appeals panels).

53. See Schkade et al., "Deliberating about Dollars," 1140–41 (showing group polarization with mock juries).

54. See Brown, *Group Processes*, 212–22, 226–45; Baron et al., "Social Corroboration and Opinion Extremity," 540.

55. See Baron et al., "Social Corroboration and Opinion Extremity," 557–59 (showing that corroboration increases confidence and hence extremism).

56. Ibid., 541, 546–47, 557 (concluding that corroboration of one's views has effects on opinion extremity).

57. See Brown, *Group Processes*, 209–11; Turner, *Rediscovering the Social Group*, 159–70; Cooper et al., "Attitudes, Norms, and Social Groups," 259, 269–70.

58. Brown, *Group Processes*, 210.

59. Ibid., 211; Cooper et al., "Attitudes, Norms, and Social Groups," 269.

60. See MacCoun, "Comparing Micro and Macro Rationality," 127–28.

61. This risk is the theme of Cass R. Sunstein, *Republic.com*.

62. See Schkade et al., "Deliberating about Dollars," 1155 (showing severity shift within juries).

63. See Brown, *Group Processes*, 220–26 (discussing group polarization).

64. See Duncan Watts, "The Kerry Cascade," available February 24, 2004, at http://slate.msn.com/id/2095993/.

65. Perspectives on skepticism vary widely. See generally David O. Brink, *Moral Realism and the Foundations of Ethics* (New York: Cambridge University Press, 1989); Gilbert Harmon and Judith Jarvis Thompson, *Moral Relativism and Moral Objectivity* (Cambridge, UK: Blackwell, 1996); John Rawls, *A Theory of Justice* (Cambridge, MA: Belknap Press, 1971), 48–53; Bernard Williams, "Interlude: Relativism," in *Morality: An Introduction to Ethics* (New York: Harper & Row, 1972), 20–26.

66. See Duncan Watts, "The Kerry Cascade" (Feb. 24, 2004), available at http://www.slate.com/id/2095993

67. See Gutmann and Thompson, *Democracy and Disagreement*, 1–9 (discussing virtues of deliberative conception of democracy).

Chapter 4 /

1. Much of the pioneering work here has been done by Robin Hanson. See, e.g., Robin Hanson, "Decision Markets," *IEEE Intelligent Systems* 14 (1999): 16; Robin Hanson, "Shall We Vote on Values, but Bet on Beliefs?" (unpublished manuscript, 2003), available at http://hanson.gmu.edu/futarchy.pdf. See generally Justin Wolfers and Eric Zitzewitz, "Prediction Markets," *Journal of Economic Perspectives* 18 (2004): 107 (valuable overview of prediction markets); Michael Abramowicz, "Prediction Markets, Administrative Decisionmaking, and Predictive Cost-Benefit Analysis," *University of Chicago Law Review* 71 (2004): 933 (recommending use of prediction markets by administrative agencies); Saul Levmore, "Simply Efficient Markets and the Role of Regulation: Lessons from the Iowa Electronic Markets and the Hollywood Stock Exchange," *Journal of Corporate Law* 28 (2003): 589; Rubet Hahn and Paul Tetlock, eds., *Information Markets* (Washington, D.C.: American Enterprise Institute, 2006).

2. See Hanson, "Shall We Vote on Values, but Bet on Beliefs?"

3. See, e.g., http://us.newsfutures.com/home/home.html.

4. But see Levmore, "Simply Efficient Markets and the Role of Regulation," 601 (showing considerable success even within quite thin markets).

5. An authoritative account is Robin Hanson, "Designing Real Terrorism Futures," August 2005, available at http://hanson.gmu.edu.

6. Ronald Bailey, "Betting on Terror: Why Futures Markets in Terror and Assassinations Are a Good Idea," *Reasononline*, July 30, 2003, http://www.reason.com/rb/rb073003.shtml.

7. Byron L. Dorgan, "The Pentagon's Ill-Conceived Market," letter to the editor, *Washington Post*, Aug. 7, 2003, A20.

8. For a replicate of the site, see "Policy Analysis Market," http://www.ratical.org/ratville/CAH/linkscopy/PAM (last visited Feb. 18, 2004).

9. See Hanson, "Designing Real Terrorism Futures."

10. For early overviews, see David M. Pennock et al., "The Real Power of Artificial Markets," *Science* 291 (2001): 987; David M. Pennock et al., *The Power of Play: Efficiency and Forecast Accuracy in Web Market Games*, NEC Research Institute Technical Report 1000–168 (2001). A wealth of valuable information can be found at http://www.chrisfmasse.com/.

11. See Joyce Berg et al., "Accuracy and Forecast Standard Error of Prediction Markets" (unpublished manuscript, July 2003), 7–10, nn. 6–7, available at http://www.biz.uiowa.edu/iem/archive/forecasting.pdf.

12. See Iowa Electronic Markets (operated by Henry B. Tippie College of Business, University of Iowa), http://www.biz.uiowa.edu/iem/markets (last visited Apr. 4, 2005).

13. See Wolfers and Zitzewitz, "Prediction Markets," 112.

14. See Robert W. Hahn and Paul C. Tetlock, *Harnessing the Power of Information: A New Approach to Economic Development*, AEI-Brookings Joint Center for Regulatory Studies, Working Paper No. 04–21 (2004), 4, available at http://www.aei-brookings.org/publications/abstract.php?pid=846.

15. See Wolfers and Zitzewitz, "Prediction Markets," 112.

16. See Erin Jordan, "Iowa Electronic Markets Yield Near-Accurate Result," *Des Moines Register*, Nov. 10, 2004, 5B.

17. Sue Kirchhoff, "Economic Predictors Don't Track Vote Results," *USA Today*, Nov. 15, 2004, 4B. Note, however, that Polly, an aggregate predictor that includes the Iowa Electronic Markets, performed even better.

18. See Berg et al., "Accuracy and Forecast Standard Error of Prediction Markets," 11–13.

19. Justin Wolfers and Andrew Leigh, "Three Tools for Forecasting Federal Elections: Lessons from 2001," *Australian Journal of Political Science* 37 (2002): 234–40.

20. See John Tierney, "Now That the Dust Has Settled," *New York Times*, Nov. 7, 2004, § 1 (National), 34.

21. Levmore, "Simply Efficient Markets and the Role of Regulation," 593.

22. Ibid.

23. See Emile Servan-Schreiber et al., "Prediction Markets: Does Money Matter?," *Electronic Markets* 14 (Sept. 2004): 3.

24. See Alexandria Sage, "Online World Bets on Jackson Trial Outcome," Reuters, May 24, 2005, available at http://news.yahoo.com/s/nm/20050524/people_nm/jackson_bets_dc/nc:720.

25. Richard Roll, "Orange Juice and Weather," *American Economic Review* 74 (1984): 871.

26. See Hanson, "Designing Real Terrorism Futures," 2.

27. See Wolfers and Zitzewitz, "Prediction Markets," 113–14.

28. Raymond D. Sauer, "The Economics of Wagering Markets," *Journal of Economic Literature* 36 (1998): 2021; S. Figlewski, "Subjective Information and Market Efficiency in a Betting Market," *Journal of Political Economy* 87 (1979): 75.

29. See Sauer, "The Economics of Wagering Markets"; the point is emphasized in Surowiecki, *The Wisdom of Crowds*, 277.

30. See Sandip Debnath et al., "Information Incorporation in Online In-Game Sports Betting Markets," *ACM Conference on Electronic Commerce* (2003), 258.

31. See Kay-Yut Chen and Charles R. Plott, *Information Aggregation Mechanisms: Concept, Design, and Implementation for a Sales Forecasting Problem*, Division of the Humanities and Social Sciences, California Institute of Technology, Social Science Working Paper No. 113 (March 2002), 3 (describing variation of this model employed by Hewlett-Packard), available at http://www.hss.caltech.edu/SSPapers/wp1131.pdf.

32. "Putting Crowd Wisdom to Work," http://googleblog.blogspot.com/2005/09/putting-crowd-wisdom-to-work.html.

33. Ibid.

34. Ibid.

35. Friedrich Hayek, "The Use of Knowledge in Society," *American Economic Review* 35 (1945): 519, reprinted in *The Essence of Hayek*, ed. Chiaki Nishiyama and Kurt Leube (Stanford: Hoover, 1984), 211. A superb treatment of Hayek's thought is Bruce Caldwell, *Hayek's Challenge: An Intellectual Biography of F. A. Hayek* (Chicago: University of Chicago Press, 2004).

36. Hayek, *The Essence of Hayek*, 212.

37. Ibid., 214.

38. Aristotle, *Politics*, trans. E. Barker (London: Oxford University Press, 1972), 123.

39. Hayek, *The Essence of Hayek*, 219–20.

40. Ibid., 220.

41. Ibid., 220–21.

42. Edmund Burke, "Reflections on the Revolution in France," in *The Portable Edmund Burke*, ed. Isaac Kramnick (New York: Penguin, 1999), 428, 443, 451.

43. For Hayek's general views on these topics, see, *Law, Legislation, and Liberty*, vol. 1 (It's "Liberty").

44. Friedrich Hayek, "The Origins and Effects of Our Morals: A Problem for Science," in *The Essence of Hayek*, 318, 330.

45. See Robert MacCoun et al., *Drug War Heresies: Learning from Other Vices, Times, and Places* (New York: Cambridge University Press, 2001).

46. *The Federalist* No. 14 (James Madison).

47. For a good overview, see Andrei Shleifer, *Inefficient Markets: An Introduction to Behavioral Finance* (Oxford: Oxford University Press, 2000).

48. See Richard Thaler, ed., *Advances in Behavioral Finance*, vol. 2 (Princeton, NJ: Princeton University Press, 2005).

49. In fact, some rigorous tests have raised doubts about it. See ibid.

50. Robert Shiller, *Irrational Exuberance*, 2d ed. (Princeton, NJ: Princeton University Press, 2005), 2, 5.

51. Ibid., 11.

52. See Erica Klarreich, "Best Guess," *Science News*, Oct. 18, 2003, 252, available at http://www.sciencenews.org/articles/20031018/bob9.asp.

53. Note, however, that Hewlett Packard produced good predictions even in a thin market. Chen and Plott, *Information Aggregation Mechanisms*, 5, 12.

54. See Abramowicz, "Prediction Markets, Administrative Decisionmaking, and Predictive Cost-Benefit Analysis," 990–92.

55. See ibid., 987–90.

56. Most dramatically, they "might have led to earlier recognition of the savings and loans crisis in the 1980s." Ibid., 988.

57. See Hahn and Tetlock, *Harnessing the Power of Information*, 3–6.

58. Ibid.

59. See Erik Snowberg et al., "Information (In)efficiency in Prediction Markets," in *Information Efficiency in Financial and Betting Markets*, ed. Leighton Vaughan Williams (Cambridge, UK: Cambridge University Press, 2005), 374.

60. See, e.g., ibid.; Hersh Shefrin, *Beyond Greed and Fear: Understanding Behavioral Finance and the Psychology of Investing* (Oxford: Oxford University Press, 1999) (exploring markets' susceptibility to cognitive errors); Shiller, *Irrational Exuberance*, 245 (discussing cognitive errors and their effects on market prices); Richard H. Thaler, ed., *Advances in Behavioral Finance* (New York: Russell Sage Foundation, 1993) (investigating effects of how investors actually behave).

61. For good discussions, see Hanson, "Designing Real Terrorism Futures," 11–14; Abramowicz, "Prediction Markets, Administrative Decisionmaking, and Predictive Cost-Benefit Analysis," 972–76.

62. Klarreich, "Best Guess," 251, 253.

63. For an overview of optimistic bias, see Christine Jolls, "Behavioral Economics Analysis of Redistributive Legal Rules," *Vanderbilt Law Review* 51 (1998): 1658–63.

64. Donald Granberg and Edward Brent, "When Prophesy Bends: The Preference-Expectation Link in U.S. Presidential Elections, 1952–1980," *Journal of Personality and Social Psychology* 45 (1983): 479.

65. See Wolfers and Zitzewitz, "Prediction Markets," 118, citing Koleman S. Strumpf, "Manipulating the Iowa Political Stock Market" (unpublished manuscript, 2004).

66. Robert Forsythe et al., "Wishes, Expectations and Actions: A Survey on Price Formation in Election Stock Markets," *Journal of Economic Behavior and Organization* 39 (1999): 94.

67. Ibid., 94–95.

68. See Charles G. Lord et al., "Biased Assimilation and Attitude Polarization: The Effects of Prior Theories on Subsequently Considered Evidence," *Journal of Personality and Social Psychology* 37 (1979): 2098. See also Muzafer Sherif and Carl I. Hovland, *Social Judgment: Assimilation and Contrast Effects in Communication and Attitude Change* (New Haven: Yale University Press, 1961), 188 (discussing manner in which individuals filter information to conform to their preexisting positions).

69. Forsythe et al., *Wishes*, 94.

70. Berg et al., "Accuracy and Forecast Standard Error of Prediction Markets," 42.

71. Forsythe et al., *Wishes*, 99–100. The term "quasi-rational" comes from Richard H. Thaler, *Quasi-Rational Economics* (New York: Russell Sage Foundation, 1991), xxi.

72. See Richard H. Thaler and William T. Ziemba, "Anomalies: Parimutuel Betting Markets: Racetracks and Lotteries," *Journal of Economic Perspectives* 2 (1988): 163 (exploring favorite–long shot bias); see also Charles F. Manski, "Interpreting the Predictions of Prediction Markets" (unpublished manuscript, Feb. 2004) (summarizing horse race data findings), available at http://faculty.econ.nwu.edu/faculty/manski/prediction_markets.pdf.

73. See David Forrest and Ian McHale, "Longshot Bias: Insights from the Betting Market on Men's Tennis," in Williams, *Information Efficiency in Financial and Betting Markets*, 215.

74. Interestingly, some sports betting shows the opposite pattern; in English professional football, long shots have been found to

be underpriced. See David Forrest and Robert Simmons, "Efficiency of the Odds on English Professional Football Matches," in Williams, *Information Efficiency in Financial and Betting Markets*, 330, 336.

75. The most important evidence can be found on Tradesports's predictions, where highly unlikely outcomes were overpriced in a number of domains. See Wolfers and Zitzewitz, "Prediction Markets," 117.

76. See Thaler, *Advances in Behavioral Finance*, vol. 2.

77. See Shiller, *Irrational Exuberance*, 2.

78. For much evidence, see Thaler, *Advances in Behavioral Finance*, vol. 2.

79. See Jordan, "Iowa Electronic Markets Yield Near-Accurate Result."

80. See Richard A. Posner, *Catastrophe: Risk and Response* (New York: Oxford University Press, 2004), 175–76 (doubting usefulness of prediction markets in context of risk of terrorism).

81. Note, however, that thin markets have proved remarkably accurate; see Levmore, "Simply Efficient Markets and the Role of Regulation," 601–3 (discussing successes of thin markets), and that some small groups might encourage outsider investors.

82. For an overview, see "FAQ: People, Julian Simon's Bet with Paul Ehrlich," Overpopulation.com, at http://www.overpopulation.com/faq/People/julian_simon.html (last visited Jan. 28, 2005).

Chapter 5 /

1. See Bol Leuf and Ward Cunningham, *The Wiki Way: Quick Collaboration on the Web* (Boston: Addison-Wesley, 2001), 15.

2. For those interested in the original WikiWikiWeb site, the place to go is http:/c2.com/cgi/wiki; it includes many thousands of pages with discussions of software design.

3. Ibid.

4. Ibid., 17.

5. All quotations from the Wikipedia site are available via http://en.wikipedia.org/wiki/Main_Page.

6. http://en.wikipedia.org/wiki/Wikipedia:Replies_to_common_ objections.

7. See http://en.wikipedia.org/wiki/Image:Stop_hand.png.

8. See http://en.wikipedia.org/wiki/Category: NPOV_disputes.

9. Taken from http://www.lessig.org/blog/archives/003012.shtml.

10. See "A Wiki For Your Thoughts" (June 17, 2005), available at http://www.latimes.com/news/printedition/opinion/la-ed-wiki17jun17,1,1789326.story.

11. See Where is the Wikitorial? (undated), available at http://www.latimes.com/news/opinion/editorials/la-wiki-splash,0,1349109.story.

12. For the full story, and the final version, see http://en.wikipedia.org/w/index.php?title=Wikipedia:Improve_this_article_about_Wikipedia&direction=next&oldid=23806738.

13. See http://www.liswiki.com/wiki/Main_Page.

14. http://www.ssrc.org/wiki/POSA/index.php?title=Main_Page.

15. See ibid.

16. http://www.worldwindcentral.com/wiki/World_Wind.

17. See "Email Is So Five Minutes Ago," *Business Week*, Nov. 28, 2005.

18. Lawrence Lessig has done a great deal of important work on the relationship between innovation and openness, in a way that is evidently influenced by the success of open source software. See Lawrence Lessig, *Free Culture* (New York: Penguin, 2005); Lawrence Lessig, *The Future of Ideas: The Fate of the Commons in a Connected World* (New York: Vintage, 2002).

19. See Peter Woodford, "Open-Source Medicine: Cure for What Ails the Third World?," available at http://www.nationalreview ofmedicine.com/issue/2004/09_23/government_medicine02_17.html.

20. See Woody Guthrie, http://en.wikipedia.org/wiki/Woody_Guthrie

21. Lawrence Lessig, "Open Source Baselines: Compared to What?," in *Government Policy toward Open Source Software*, ed. Robert Hahn et al. (Washington, DC: Brookings, 2002), 50.

22. Ibid., 53.

23. GNU General Public License (vol. 2, 1991), § 2©, available at http://www.opensource.org/licenses/gpl-license.php.

24. Strong copyleft licenses, and the GPL specifically, are commonly used in the open source community: Of the 65,439 open source projects hosted by SourceForge.net, fully 45,151, or 68.9 percent, use the GPL (SourceForge.net. figures as of July 22, 2005). SourceForge.net is a large host service for open source projects. These numbers refer only to those projects licensed under an Open Source Initiative approved license. There is an intense debate about whether people use the GPL because they like copyleft or, instead, because many other people use it, and users do not want to have to deal with a large number of different licenses.

25. Common forms of this license include the Lesser General Public License and the Mozilla Public License (MPL). The MPL provides that the open source code may be included in a larger work. Mozilla Public License 1.1 § 3.7.

26. Raymond, *The Cathedral and the Bazaar*, 30.

27. I draw here on the extremely illuminating discussion in Steven Weber, *The Success of Open Source* (Cambridge, MA: Harvard University Press, 2004), 171–78.

28. http://groups.google.com/group/comp.os.minix/msg/2194d253268b0a1b; quoted in ibid., 54–55.

29. Ibid., 55.

30. Interested readers may enjoy Torvalds's homepage; see http://www.cs.helsinki.fi/u/torvalds/.

31. See Richard Stallman, "The GNU Operating System and the Free Software Movement," in *Open Sources: Voices from the Open Source Revolution*, ed. Chris Dibona et al. (Sebastopol, CA: O'Reilly, 1999), 55–56.

32. Ibid., 57.

33. See Josh Lerner and Jean Tirole, "The Economics of Technology Sharing: Open Source and Beyond," *Journal of Economic Perspectives* 19 (2005): 100.

34. Ibid.

35. See Raymond, *The Cathedral and the Bazaar*.

36. Ibid., 21–22.

37. Here, too, I am grateful to Ethan Zuckerman for clarifying comments.

38. Eric Raymond, "Homesteading the Noosphere," in *The Cathedral and the Bazaar*, 67, 81, 110.

39. Ibid., 89.

40. I borrow here from Weber, *The Success of Open Source*, 185–89.

41. About the Mozilla Foundation, see http://www.mozilla.org/foundation/.

42. This information was obtained through the Bonsai tool provided by Mozilla.org for keeping track of changes to the code and running a search for changes between the specified times. See http://bonsai.mozilla.org/cvsqueryform.cgi?

43. Weber, *The Success of Open Source*, 188.

44. Ibid., 187.

45. See "An Open-Source Shot in the Arm?," *The Economist*, June 10, 2004.

46. See http://rsss.anu.edu.au/~janeth/home.html.

47. "Plant Biotech Goes Open Source," Feb. 10, 2005, http://news.bbc.co.uk/1/hi/sci/tech/4248155.stm.

48. Ibid.

49. Ibid.

50. See Stephen Breyer, "The Uneasy Case for Copyright," *Harvard Law Review* 84 (1970): 281; William Landes and Richard Posner, "An Economic Analysis of Copyright Law," *Journal of Legal Studies* 18 (1989): 325; Lawrence Lessig, *Free Culture: How Big Media Uses Technology and the Law to Lock Down Culture and Control Creativity* (New York: Penguin, 2004).

51. Taken from an interview (2003) with Christopher Lydon at http://blogs.law.harvard.edu/lydon/2003/07/31, summarized at the same location.

52. Hugh Hewitt, *Blog: Understanding the Information Reformation That's Changing Your World* (Nashville, TN: Thomas Nelson, 2005).

53. Ibid., 42.

54. Ibid., 36.

55. http://www.becker-posner-blog.com/archives/2004/12/introduction_to_1.html.

56. Lada Adamic and Natalie Glance, "The Political Blogosphere and the 2004 Election: Divided They Blog," 2005, 4, http://www.blogpulse.com/papers/2005/AdamicGlanceBlog WWW.pdf.

57. Eszter Hargittai, Jason Gallo, and Matt Kane, "Mapping the Political Blogosphere: Analysis of Large-Scale Online Political Discussion" (unpublished manuscript, 2005).

58. "FAQ: Metamoderation," http://slashdot.org/faq/metamod.shtml.

59. See Nathanial Poor, "Mechanisms of an Online Public Sphere: The Website Slashdot, Journal of Computer-Mediated Communication," 2005, http://jcmc.indiana.edu/vol10/issue2/poor.html.

60. See Lior Strahilevitz, "'How Am I Driving?' *For Everyone*," May 16, 2006, available at http://uchicagolaw.typepad.com/faculty/2006/05/hows_my_driving.html.

Chapter 6 /

1. See Jeffrey A. Sonnenfeld, "What Makes Great Boards Great," *Harvard Business Review* (Sept. 2002).

2. Ibid.

3. See Luther Gulick, *Administrative Reflections from World War II* (Birmingham: University of Alabama Press, 1948), 120–25, 120, 121.

4. Ibid., 125.

5. Stasser and Titus, "Hidden Profiles," 309.

6. Angela Hung and Charles Plott, "Information Cascades: Replication and an Extension to Majority Rule and Conformity-Rewarding Institutions," *American Economic Review* 91 (2001): 1515.

7. See Christensen and Abbott, "Team Medical Decision Making," 272–76.

8. Ibid.

9. See Ridgeway, "Social Status and Group Structure," in Hogg and Tindale, *Group Processes*, 54.

10. Stasser and Titus, "Hidden Profiles," 308.

11. Ibid.

12. Ibid.

13. Ibid.

14. See Gene Rowe and George Wright, "Expert Opinions in Forecasting: The Role of the Delphi Technique," in *Principle of Forecasting*, ed. J. Scott Armstrong (Boston: Kluwer Academic Publishers, 2001), 126.

15. See ibid., 130; Hastie, "Review Essay," 139.

16. See Hastie, "Review Essay," 139–45.

17. Ibid., 129.

18. Ibid., 129–30.

19. See Gustafson et al., "A Comparative Study of Differences in Subjective Likelihood Estimates."

20. Janis, *Groupthink*, 268.

21. Gary Katzenstein, "The Debate on Structured Debate: Toward a Unified Theory," *Organizational Behavior and Human Decision Processes* 66 (1996): 317–18.

22. Alexander L. George and Eric K. Stern, "Harnessing Conflict in Foreign Policy Making: From Devil's to Multiple Advocacy," *Presidential Studies Quarterly* 32 (2002): 486.

23. Ibid.

24. Ibid.

25. See Garold Stasser, "The Uncertain Role of Unshared Information in Collective Choice," in *Shared Cognition in Organization: The Management of Knowledge*, ed. Leigh L. Thompson et al. (Mahwah, NJ: Erlbaum, 1999), 56–57.

26. See Stasser and Titus, "Hidden Profiles," 308 (citing studies showing that "when the bearer of unique information was labeled an expert, the group seemingly paid more attention to the information"); Garold Stasser et al., "Expert Roles and Information Exchange During Discussion: The Importance of Knowing Who Knows What," *Journal of Experimental Social*

Psychology 31 (1995): 248–49, 256 (showing that assigning expert roles led to more discussion of unshared data).

27. See Stasser et al., "Expert Roles and Information Exchange During Discussion," 248–49.

28. Stasser and Titus, "Hidden Profiles," 310 (summarizing studies).

29. See Christopher Edley, "A U.S. Watchdog for Civil Liberties," *Washington Post*, July 14, 2002, B7.

30. The 9/11 Commission, citing the lack of a "voice within the executive branch" designed to consider liberty concerns, has made a similar recommendation. See National Commission on Terrorist Attacks upon the U.S., *The 9/11 Commission Report*, 2004, 395, available at http://www.gpoaccess.gov/911/index.html.

31. See Ackerman and Hassler, *Clean Coal/Dirty Air*, 79–86.

Index /